THE ROCK REPORT

FLETCHER A. BROTHERS

STARBURST PUBLISHERS

TM

P.O. Box 4123, Lancaster, Pennsylvania 17604

Fletcher A. Brothers, a hard hitting matter-of-fact preacher with a love for 'kids' is the founder of Freedom Village USA, one of the largest homes for troubled young people in America. As an outgrowth of this ministry, God has opened the doors for daily and weekly TV programs, daily radio programs, a Bible College, and several other evangelistic outreaches. In 1987 Freedom village of Canada was opened. Brothers' goal is to reach every teenager in America and Canada with the message of hope through Jesus Christ. Address inquiries to Rev. Fletcher Brothers, Freedom Village, P. O. Box 146, Lakemont, New York 14857.

Credits:

Cover Art by Kerne Erickson.

THE ROCK REPORT

Copyright © 1987 by Starburst, Inc.
All rights reserved.

For information and permission address: Starburst, Inc., P.O. Box 4123, Lancaster, PA 17604

First Printing   (October, 1987)
Second Printing   (October, 1988)

ISBN: 0-914984-13-6
Library of Congress Catalog Number 87-91288

Printed in the United States of America

Dedication

To Teens and their families everywhere—
God loves you and so do I!

A very special thank you to Scott Ziegler whose hours and hours of research have made this book possible. To Pastor Oz Adams, Pastor Rick Jones and Miss Claudia Woods who assisted Scott in the research. To Mrs. Terry Jackson for her special assistance in organizing, editing and hours of typing. And then to the young people of Freedom Village—who are the real proof there is a victory.

Pastor Brothers

CONTENTS

PREFACE VII

INTRODUCTION IX

THE FOUR M'S 13

THE GROUPS 19

SYMBOLISM AND THE OCCULT 95

WHAT THE VICTIMS SAY 133

DOES THE BIBLE HAVE ANYTHING TO SAY
ABOUT ROCK AND ROLL? 139

Preface

The Evidence Demands a Verdict.

The Bible in *Hosea 4:6* says, *My people are destroyed for lack of knowledge: because thou hast rejected knowledge, I will also reject thee . . . seeing thou hast forgotten the law of thy God, I will also forget thy children.*

Rock music has changed dramatically over recent years. Sado-masochism, Satan worship and blatant vulgarity are a long way from "Elvis' pelvis" which enraged those of his day.

But you say, "Wait a minute, Pastor Brothers . . . not all rock groups sing about filth and occult themes or sing the praises of rebellion, drugs and suicide."

Exactly! And that's why we have prepared this *"Rock Report."* We felt it was time for a "handbook" on rock groups and individual singers so that with this basic information young and old alike could avoid being *destroyed for lack of knowledge.* During my years of working with young people, time and time again they have admitted to me that they were unaware of where they were being led by the music themes of certain singers and groups—that is, not until they were caught in the *spider's web.* Young people need to be informed about those who claim "Satanic help or Satanic powers" or admit to alternative lifestyles.

Parents are confused. Where do they go to keep up with today's music? They are constantly coming to us saying, "Who in the world is this group . . . or what kind of music do they sing or play . . . what is their theme?" Now, with the *"Rock Report"*, they can find the answers to many of these questions.

The *"Rock Report"* is in no way conclusive. New groups appear and "new waves" hit the market almost daily. For this reason, depending upon the number of new groups, we will give you a regular update—annually or semi-annually.

We have also determined that this be a "report" . . . not just a book on rock. There are a few thoughts shared of course, but first and foremost, the *"Rock Report"* is designed to give you a quick, ready reference guide to many of today's rock musicians. There are some groups that have been omitted, some intentionally, others because by the time the typewriters stop and the manuscript goes to press new groups have appeared.

Rock music is here to stay. As it has in the past, it's main emphasis will vary, but realistically . . . it's going to live on. The *"Rock Report"* will follow trends and events which are here today and will be here tomorrow . . . rock and roll!

Our prayer is that the information in this book will help you make a more intelligent decision about what you will and will not listen to. If you are a parent, this *"Rock Report"* will provide the information you need to make intelligent decisions about the kind of music you permit to influence your young person's mind. Let the evidence we have provided help you decide your own verdict!

Introduction

Why such a big deal over my music?

Whenever I speak on Rock music and announce the title, almost invariably, somebody gets upset. I know what's going on in their mind, I've heard it many times before. They say, "This preacher just doesn't like my style of music, therefore, he preaches against it. I wish he would leave it alone—it's just music."

Let me be honest with you: (1) I don't preach against rock and roll because I don't like it. It just so happens that in the flesh, I love it! At the time I was "saved" I got rid of literally hundreds of dollars worth of albums. I have to admit, it still appeals to me. But so does blackberry brandy. But I do not drink it! I do not preach against rock and roll because I do not like it, I preach against it because I know what it involves. I've done thousands of hours of research into it, not to mention the effect that I saw it make on my own life.

(2) Rock and roll is not just music. It's much more than that. Musicians of other styles do not have the cult type following of rock and roll. Kevin Cronin from *REO Speedwagon* said, "We have a cult of three million people following us." There are teenagers that would literally kill over their rock. The artists are gods to them. *Rock and roll is more than just music, it is religion.*

Ozzy Osbourne sang, "Rock and Roll is my religion." In an interview he said, "Rock and roll is a religion in itself." When Leon Russel was asked several years ago what a good alternative to Christianity would be, he replied, "The religion of rock and roll." Blackie Lawless of *W.A.S.P.* said, "I look at rock like a religion." (Faces, 2/85, p.53) *KISS* sang in *God of Thunder*, *"I gather darkness to please me, and I command you to kneel before the god of thunder, the god of rock and roll."* When *Judas Priest* wsa asked about the title of their album, *Defender's of the Faith*, they replied, "We're defending the faith of heavy metal music."

In fact, many musicians and fans look upon concerts as religious or church services, not just entertainment. Patrick Anderson from the *Milwaukee Journal Magazine* said, "That's the real reason for either rock or country concerts, they're the religious ceremonies of a non-religious age." Craig Chaquito of *Starship* said, *"Rock concerts are the churches of today."* *Iron Maiden* opened concerts during one tour with the words, "Welcome to Satan's Sanctuary." Brian Wilson of the *Beach Boys* said, "We feel it's our responsibility, partially, to carry the maharishi message into the world." John Denver said, "As a self appointed messiah, I view music as far more than just entertainment." He went on to tell of the fact that he felt it was a tool to promote his new secular religion. Talking about Billy Squier, *Circus* magazine said, "Now Billy Squier is taking the gospel to America and Europe, preaching his own rock sermons in sold-out concerts." *Blue Oyster Cult* has an album entitled *On Your Feet or On Your Knees*. The front side of the album pictures a church scene. The backside of the album pictures a person wearing black leather gloves reading what appears to be a Bible. Wearing black leather gloves is a practice in the Satanic Church when they read their unholy scriptures. The inside of the album cover pictures the band performing on a church platform with all those in attendance wearing black hooded garments.

Meatloaf's John Steinman said, "I've always been fascinated by the "supernatural" and always felt rock was the perfect idiom for it." He went on to tell how he believes that he gets possessed when on stage. Marc Storace, the vocalist for *Krokus*, said this while talking about the unusual appeal of hard rock among young people, "It's a ritual and has—believe it or not—a spiritual context to it . . . ." (Creem, 3/85, p.64) Sting, the lead singer of the *Police* said, "The pure essence of music is very spiritual . . . ." The father of the founder of *Rolling Stones*, Brian Jones, told interviewer Stanley Booth that music was Brian's religion. (*Dance with the Devil*, Stanley Booth, Random House, 1984, p.109) Legendary heavy metal inspirer Jimi Hendrix said, "I used to go to Sunday School but the only thing I believe in now is music." (*Jimi*, Curtis Knight, Praeger Pub., NY, 1974)

So you see, rock and roll is not just music. It is a very dangerous religion. Veteran rocker David Bowie said, "Rock has always been the devil's music, you can't convince me that it isn't. I honestly believe everything I've said—I believe rock and roll is dangerous."

We're not attempting to take away something from you just because we don't like it ourselves. We wrote this book out of a genuine concern for you and your future. We have seen first hand, time and time again, how this 'religion' has caught up young people and destroyed their lives.

Enough of what we have to say. We'll let the groups speak for themselves.

SCOTT ZIEGLER

The Four M's

What's wrong with Rock Music?

I make no apology when I say that I believe that rock music, and in particular the recent heavy metal form that I call "murder music" and "music pornography", is public enemy number one of our young people today. Bear in mind that every day I deal with the broken lives of teenagers. *From experience, I can tell you that rock music is one of the major factors in the downfall of today's young people.* Rarely have I taken a young person into Freedom Village (a home for troubled young people) who, to varying degrees, has not been involved with rock music.

When asked what is wrong with rock music, I'm sure you can understand my temptation to answer, "Everything!" In fact, I can't think of one good thing to come out of the recent trend in rock music other than the revenue it provides to our free enterprise system. But even this is not worth the price in teenage lives. If you faced, every day as I do, the broken lives, burned out minds from drug use, the aftermath of suicide attempts, occultism, and so on, I'm sure you would agree . . . the price is too high!

Knowing that my "everything" answer will be too general for some, and for others no amount of explanation will convince them of the dangers, I would like you to look at what I call *The Four M's of rock music.*

The Music

It is a proven fact that music moves people. Music causes an increase or slowing down of activity. It can put you to sleep or wake you up. It can either soothe or irritate. Music plays a very important role in day to day life. The next time you go to the dentist ask him why he always plays soft easy listening music. Or the next time you are watching a "thriller" movie on TV—listen to the music— the eerie sounds they play right before the "good guy" is about to get hit over the head by the "bad guy." Can you imagine Dee Snider and *Twisted Sister* screaming in the background, "We ain't gonna take it any more?"

Certain music produces specific results. You have been out driving and one of those up-tempo songs comes on and before you know it there are red lights flashing in your rear view mirror. Now how are you going to explain to the officer that "the music made me do it?"

Yes, music affects us and the beat affects us. As you read through this book you will notice that the rock stars themselves realize *the "beat" is sensual, arousing, and can be used to generate frenzy.* Much of "heavy metal" is void of words. Long sections of the songs are often given a "beat" designed for a violent, near frenzy response from listeners. One would not expect people to pound on each other or cut each other with razor blades to "easy listening" music.

I can remember, several years ago, counseling a young man whose problem was rebellion. (This was before punk rock came into existence.) His parents were broken hearted and at their wits end. They finally convinced him to talk me. He had shoulder length hair, wore an earring, a rock tee-shirt and had the letters "K I S S" tattooed on the fingers of each hand. Now I know *KISS* is "old stuff" today, but at that time *KISS* were his idols. During our conversations he told me that if it came down to a choice between his parents and rock and roll, he'd take rock and roll. "In fact, man, I've sold my soul to rock and roll. It's my life." When I asked him what there was about it that pulled him to it he said, *"It's the beat, man, the beat. It gets inside me and I just have to follow it."* The last contact I had concerning him, he had dropped out of school, was living on the streets and had almost died after drinking a fifth of vodka while already high on marijuana.

I wonder how many teens have gone to early graves "following the beat."

The Musicians

Rock stars today have become the "idols", "role models" and "patterns" for teenagers. In and of itself, this is not a shocking fact or a new phenomenon. To any adult who ever wore saddle shoes or a duck tail haircut, there is little room for argument.

The *Beatles* took the world by storm. An entire generation was captivated by this one group. But what kind of example did they set and what kind is being set by today's rock stars? A quick glance at the list on pages 141—143 tells how some of the most famous rock stars have died and will in itself give cause for alarm.

Time and again I have heard it said that the rock stars are only responding to the demands of the teenagers. I strongly disagree with this. The rock stars are creating the demand . . . then filling it. They set the stage. They set the beat. They create the fad and then say "come follow us." But where are they leading? They do not even pretend to present a wholesome, Christian life. Instead, they openly admit to lifestyles of drugs, free sex, rebellion, the occult, homosexuality and the "highway to hell."

Agreed, not every group follows this pattern and some even deplore the actions of their peers. But the fact remains that they are role models for our young people.

How far will teenagers follow their "idols?" One seventeen year old boy from North Carolina followed his idols, *The Scorpions*, all the way to a bridge on I-40 and "flew over the rainbow" as one of their songs advocated. *The suicide note found on the seat of his car read, "Tell the Scorpions their number one fan has flown to the rainbow."*

How many of the 500,000 kids who tried to kill themselves last year were influenced by their "idols?" Even if they were "mental cripples" as the rock stars and their supporters claim, do the rock stars have the right to drive them over the edge?

The Message

What is the message of rock music? In the words of the stars and their fans . . . sex, drugs and rock and roll. Let's pretend that we decided to take away all the songs that deal with free sex, homosexuality, rebellion, Satan, the occult, murder, suicide, incest, vulgarity, sado-masochism, anti-patriotic themes and violence . . . what would be left? Very little.

You may say, "that's censorship!" There has always been and still is a form of censorship. The question is not whether to censor or not to censor but just where do we draw the line? It used to be that the words "hell" and "damn" could not be uttered on the airwaves. But today they are used all the time. We moved our standards but there are still words and acts that cannot be televised.

While in Washington attending the hearings on rock music, I was interviewed by a reporter from *ABC*. The lady asked if I was in favor of censorship. I replied, "Yes, when it comes to music that tells a young person to kill people or influences them to commit suicide or the music is pornographic." The reporter came back with, *"But you must realize that censorship is against the First Amendment of the Constitution. How dare you even advocate something like that?"* I handed her a sheet of paper containing the lyrics to several top songs of the day and asked her to read them over the air. She told me that she could not. When pushed for a reason why she couldn't, she said that she was not allowed to use those words on the air. You see, *she* was being censored. As I said before, there will always be censorship. But how far will we allow it to go before we draw the line and say "no more?"

If you will look at the downhill trend in morals of our young people and the rise in the number of teen suicides, drug addiction, sexual permissiveness, venereal disease and the trend in current rock music, surely you will realize the effect it has on our young people.

The Mutation

What's wrong with rock music? The beat and it's stimulations. The musicians and their lifestyles. The message. But more importantly the "mutation" or what it does to our young people. I have said it before but now say it again as we discuss what rock music and its influence produces in our young people . . . *the evidence demands a verdict!*

We are producing many rebellious, drug and alcohol addicted, amoral young people. Many in this generation are broken, disillusioned, hopeless teens. They are being forced to "grow up" at 9, 10 and 11 years of age and to deal with promiscuity, drugs, crime, incest, etc. They have not been allowed to experience the innocence of childhood. For many of them life is over at age 15 or 16.

Rock stars are saying they have nothing to do with all the problems kids are having. They say that the kids who are killing themselves while listening to "suicide music" are the ones who are gassing themselves in their cars leaving notes containing the lyrics to the morbid, "end it all" type music were mental cripples anyway. But I ask, "What gives the musician the right to push them over the edge?"

I have spoken with several musicians "off the record" and though they publicly defend their industry, privately they are disgusted with many of the new heavy metal, "let me show you how raunchy I can be" groups!

Again I say, the evidence demands a verdict! Before you say that rock music does not affect young people go to the next concert in your area . . . sit in a shopping mall and observe the young people for a little while . . . then if you still say "No way. It doesn't affect kids" talk to a parent whose young person is addicted to rock music.

If a man woke up to drink, drank all day long, carried a bottle on his hip with a straw attached to his mouth and went to bed with a bottle, we'd say that man was a drunk! Like I said . . . "the evidence demands a verdict!"

THE GROUPS

What they themselves claim to be.

AC/DC - According to Circus magazine, *AC/DC* means 'bisexual.' The group *Sweet* had a song entitled *AC/DC* on their album *Demolition Boulevard*. It was about a bisexual woman. *AC/DC* is well known for their strong occultic themes. They have a song entitled, *Hell ain't a Bad Place to Be*. The song *Hell's Bells* says, *"See my light flashin' as I split the night, cause if God's on the left, then I'm stickin' to the right! . . . I'm gonna take ya to hell . . . I'm gonna get 'cha—Satan got 'cha . . . If God's on the left, I'm on the right. If you're into evil, you're a friend of mine."* One album is entitled, *Highway to Hell*. It contains the song *Highway to Hell*. Bon Scott, who was the lead singer of the group at that time, screamed out into a microphone at the gyrating fans, *"Ain't nothin' I'd rather do, going down for the last time, my friends are gonna be there too, I'm on a highway to hell (repeat) . . . Hey Momma, look at me, I'm going to the promised land. Hey Satan, paid my dues, playing in a rocking band. I'm on a highway to hell! (repeat)"* Shortly after cutting this album, and directly after singing that song, Bon Scott went on an all night drinking binge and the next morning was found dead in a friend's car. He had choked to death on his own vomit. Mr. Scott may have gone to the place

AC/DC

he was singing about but found it was not the promised land and the 'good time party' that he thought it was going to be. Incidentally, why did he sing, *"Hey Satan, paid my dues, playing in a rockin' band?"* If there's nothing wrong with rock and roll, why did Bon Scott feel that he was doing the devil a favor and that he had earned his way to hell? Because Rock is one of the devil's most effective tools to reach and control teenagers, and Bon Scott knew it! Angus Young, the lead guitarist for the group, is called the "guitar demon." He said this: *"By the time we're halfway through the first number someone else is steering me—I'm just along for the ride. I become possessed when I get on stage."* (Hit Parader, 7/85)

Accept - They have an album entitled, *Balls to the Wall*. It contains quite a bit of explicit sex, including, *Turn Me On. "I can't wait to get you down on the dirty floor . . . please turn me on, I can't hold it . . . Please turn me on, I explode . . . It would be good to do it in a nice way but sorry, I just got no time."* Screaming for a Love Bite from *Metal Heart* says, *"Screaming for a love bite . . . It's black and blue and it happened to you . . . It hurts just the first time . . . ."*

Abbitoir - This is not a mainline group (probably partially due to the fact that their music and literature is full of obscenities that are banned in this country). One album is entitled, *Vicious Attack*. The cover pictures a nude woman with a meat hook pressing against her breast.

Aerosmith

Aerosmith - Manager David Krebbs said, "When you're in a certain frame of mind, particularly sexually orientated, there's nothing better than Rock and Roll because that's where most of the performers are at." (Circus, 10/17/78, p.34)

Animotion

Animotion - They have a song entitled, *Obsession*, where they sing, *"You are my obsession, I am obsessed with you . . . what you want me to be for you to sleep with me."*

Beastie Boys - This is one of the hottest new groups around. Just a few years ago they were booed off stage when opening for a Madonna tour (USA Today, 1/27/87), but today they are filling auditoriums to capacity wherever they go. They are introducing America to a brand new style of music, crossing black rap with white punk/heavy metal. Their debut album, *Licensed to Ill*, which is already a top ten seller, has the group saying, *"Bein' bad news is what we're all about."* They're telling the truth. The album, along with their concerts, is filled with profanity. They seem particularly fond of words starting with the letter 'F.' Newsweek recently told of their interviewing habit of spicing "almost every sentence with obscenities." The magazine also said: "Among other things, the *Boys* lustily exclaim the joys of girls, gunplay and getting high— a frosty brew and angel dust are the drugs of choice in their lyrics." (Newsweek, 2/2/87, p.70) The group is such a breakthrough because they are all white, yet they have a tremendous black following. The traditional black rap is now crossing into the mainstream of society and its lyrics are getting dirtier than ever with this set of brawlers.

Black Sabbath - The term *Black Sabbath* comes from an actual holiday that occurs in the calendar of the Satanic church. One of their album titles is actually a description of how they got their fame, *We Sold Our Soul for Rock and Roll*. In *Hit Parader*, Ozzy Osbourne (the original leader of the group, now gone solo) tells how the band came to fame. Initially, they were a group of working class kids that played hand me down tunes. It was not until members of the group got into the occult that they grew popular. (Hit Parader, 2/85, p.42) They are not playing a game. They meant it when they said, "We sold our soul for rock and roll." Another album is entitled, *Sabbath Bloody Sabbath*. The cover of this album appears to portray an actual human sacrifice! All those on the drawing are in the nude just as it is in an actual Satanic service. A 666 is located toward the top of the cover. Here are a portion of the words to the song *N.I.B.* (Nativity In Black): *"Now I have you with me under my power. Our love grows stronger now with every hour. Look into my eyes, you'll see who I am, my name is Lucifer, please take my hand."* The group disbanded temporarily. When they came back together they put out a new album and called it, *Born Again*. A baby demon is pictured on the cover. The group has given birth to both Ozzy Osbourne and Ronnie James Dio.

Blessed Death - The title song to their album of the same name as the band is a prayer for death, an encouragement for suicide. *"Take me blessed death. Give me blessed death. Free me blessed death. Save me blessed death."*

Blue Oyster Cult - The *B.O.Cult*, as they are called by their fans, take as the symbol for the band an ancient marking which combined the question mark and the cross to symbolize the questioning of the cross of Christ. The album cover to *On Your Feet or On Your Knees* pictures a church on the front cover. On the backside is a picture of a black leather book with a thin ribbon marker inside (made to appear like a Bible), being read by someone wearing black leather gloves. (This is practiced in the Satanic Church when they read their unholy scriptures.) The inside of the cover pictures the band performing on what appears to be a church platform. They are performing in front of a crowd of creatures all dressed in black hooded garments. *Blue Oyster Cult* looks upon their concerts as church services, as many rock musicians do. (*Iron Maiden* opened concerts with the words, "Welcome to Satan's Sanctuary.") The album *Some Enchanted Evening* pictures the tarot card's depiction of the Grim Reaper (the devil's angel of death) on the cover. The album contains the song *Don't Fear the Reaper* which encourages suicide. *Agents of Fortune* shows a magician holding tarot card's spread out in his fingers. The cards spell the message, "He who comes against the power faces death." With his other hand, the magician is pointing to the group's anti-christ symbol. Another song, *You're not the One*, contains a high speed subliminal message that says, "*And furthermore our father is not in heaven.*"

Bon Jovi

Bon Jovi - This band will some day be hailed as one of the all time most popular hard rock bands. Considered to be a heavy metal group, they first took the rock world by storm with *7800° Farenheit*. Their third album however, *Slippery When Wet* (a title claimed to be 'deliberately provocative' by *Rock Express* magazine), has proved to be their most popular yet, being at the time of this writing the number one selling album in the United States. With it, they have become history's fourth hard rock band to join such ranks. Headbangers are pleased because the album has added more 'heavy metal' to the airwaves. (Rock Express, 1/87, p.15) Where did they get the title *Slippery When Wet*? Jon Bon Jovi tells us: "The title came from hanging around this strip bar one day . . . . We kept drinking, and there was this girl dancing, *In and Out of Love* . . . . So she's taking a shower and we're getting drunk and upset about the cover shots at the same time. We're looking ar her all wet, and the idea kind of surfaced in our mind at the same time . . . . So we got away with that but we couldn't get the cover we wanted. The record company thought it would upset the *Mothers Against Rock*." (Rock Express, 1/87. p.15, 37) The album holds true to the sex induced title. Besides the wet scantily dressed girls on the inner sleeve, the lyrics also contain it. In *Without Love* they open the song with a verse about a prostitute. *Raise Your Hands* says: "*You—you got a nasty reputation . . . Well now that we're together, Show me what you can do, You're under the gun . . . .*" Another song is entitled, *Social Disease*. Although the song is not about V.D., young people know what they're referring to. In *Never Say Goodbye* they sing of a girlfriend losing her virginity in the back seat of a car. In *Wild in the Streets* they sing, "*A member of the boy's brigade had a date with the girl next door. You know it made her daddy crazy but it only made her want him more . . . So she headed out thru her bathroom window. What her daddy didn't know was gonna be alright.*" Where did this poor overprotected girl wind up? The song tells us, "*Making love in the backseat.*" Probably losing the same thing that the girl in *Never Say Goodbye* lost. And this, at the time of writing, is the most popular album in the country!

David Bowie

David Bowie - Though David Bowie does not seem to be on the forefront of the Rock scene, *Time* magazine said that he is the most influential of all the individuals in Rock today. He toured America in 1983 and sold out stadiums all across the land. He is the trend setter in Rock and Roll. He was the first to come out and admit to the press that he was "gay." He was one of the first to wear feminine make up on stage. He was the first to delve into the glitter rock movement which was the forerunner of today's punk rock. He also was the first to release what became known as disco music. (Time, 7/18/83) That is something to think about when you consider this quote from him: "Rock has always been the devil's music. You can't convince me that it isn't. I honestly believe everything that I've said—I believe Rock and Roll is dangerous." (Rolling Stone, 2/12/76, p.83) Years ago, David married a model by the name of Angela Barnett. He said that he met her while they were "laying the same bloke." (Time, 7/18/83) In other words, they met while having sex with the same man. David and Angela had a live-in friend by the name of Tony Visconti. This is what Tony said life with David and Angela was like: "Thursday night was gay night. David would go to a gay club, Angie to a lesbian club, and they would bring home people they found. We had to lock our bedroom door because these people they brought back home with them would come climbing into new beds looking for fresh blood." (Time, 7/18/83, p.58) If that is what life with the most influential rocker is like, is it any wonder that rock has degenerated to the place where it is today? His queer lifestyle is not limited to home, He also has been known to commit homosexual acts with his lead guitarist, Mick Ronson, on stage during concert! (Time, 7/18/83, p.57) One of his most recent songs is entitled, *Underground*. The song talks about a place underground that lasts forever. It seems to be talking about hell. Only Bowie does not describe it as a place where *the worm dieth not and the fire is not quenched*. He makes the place look desirable. He says your *"daddy"* (Jesus said, *ye are of your father the devil*) can take you there and it is a place where *"nothing hurts again . . . a land serene, a crystal moon."* He says it is for the *"lost"*, and there you will find *"someone true."* *Circus* magazine reported that recently he has been working with Iggy Pop for Iggy's newest album.

The Cars - This pop band has done their best to maintain a sexual image. They feature scantily dressed woman on album covers and promo material. One song is entitled, *Lust for Kicks*. That title is self explanatory. Here are words to the song *You're All I've Got Tonight*, *"You can pump me, I don't care. You can bump me, I don't care. You can love me just about everywhere."*

Eric Clapton - Many a casual London traveler has noticed graffiti in the city that says, "Eric Clapton is god." The craze has come out of the ever existing argument as to who is the best guitarist in the world. Some consider Clapton to be. One of his album titles sounded very spiritual. It was called, *In the Presence of the Lord*. Yet that very album had a second cover featuring a teenage girl nude from the waist up. Clapton said that the title song was about a place where he was safe from police to do drugs. Another song was entitled, *Cocaine*. Another very popular one was, *Lay Down Sally*. The words match the title's suggestiveness.

Alice Cooper - This is a man. His real name is Vincent Furnier. He changed his name to Alice Cooper because he is possessed by a seventeenth century witch by the name of Alice Cooper. He met her at a seance and she promised him world fame in exchange for the possession of his body. (Rock 'n' Roll and the Occult, Harrisburg, PA) To see one of Cooper's concerts would leave little doubt in one's mind that he is possessed. One of his favorite antics on stage is to whack off the heads of live looking baby manikins. When he would do so, blood would squirt from the infant's head and torso. He then would drag the remains around stage, leaving behind a trail of blood. His earlier albums include, *Alice Cooper Goes to Hell, Welcome to my Nightmare,* and *Killer*. The song, *Looney Tune,* is about suicide. *In Hallowed be My Name* he sings, *"Screaming at mothers, cursing the Bible, hallowed be my name."* Another of his songs is entitled, *Second Coming*. The lyrics to that one contain these words, *"So have no gods before me. I'm the light. The devil's getting smarter all the time."* Most of his songs are sexually explicit, including songs about necrophilia (sex with a corpse) such as, *I Love the Dead,* and *Cold Ethyl*. Here are the words to the latter: *"One thing I miss is Cold Ethyl and her kiss. We met last night making love by the refrigerator light. Ethyl, Ethyl let me squeeze you in my arms. Ethyl, Ethyl come and freeze me with your charms. One thing no lie, Ethyl's frigid as an eskimo pie.*

She's cool in bed. She oughta' be 'cuz Ethyl's dead." While Cooper has not been in the limelight these last few years, he has just released a new album. It is entitled *Constrictor* and it is full of sex. The song, *Give It Up* was written to criticize the girl who waits to have sex. *Thrill My Gorilla* says: *"We lay on our skins, original sins. AH, ah,ah,ah. We touch, we feel, we scream, we squeel. Thrill my gorilla . . . ."* The song, *Trick Bag* is about sado-masochism. In *Crawlin'* he sings, *"Your dress is hangin' on a hook on the door. My jeans are lying in a pile on the floor. Flat on my back, trying to catch my breath. When we were rockin' tonight I thought we were gonna rock to death . . . Your hair is tangled and your lipstick is gone. You're stretched out calling my name with just your heels on . . . ."* This perversion is all from one album and it contains much more. If Alice Cooper is back, his morals have not changed one bit!

Elvis Costello - Mr. Costello is a constant reemerging figure in Rock and Pop. He said this, "Rock 'n' roll has a potential for evil—far beyond any conception of it as 'the Devil's music' . . . ." (Musician, 2/87, p.56)

Coven - The word coven means "a gathering of witches." This group recorded an actual black mass and released it as a song. At the onset could be heard a string of bells, sounding like funeral bells. Afterward were chants in Latin. Then a voice with these words broke through, *"Do you renounce Jesus as the Christ?"* In its day, the group held only mild popularity but they were the forerunners of the saturation of Satanism today on the rock scene.

Culture Club - For years Boy George was advertised by the press as being a drug free rocker. He was trusted by mothers around the world because he 'spoke out'

Culture Club

against drugs at his concerts. However, his recent drug scandals have silenced those claims. Boy George was a hypocrite. Perhaps worse than this, he is an admitted gay and dresses like a female much of the time. Boy George and his perverted ideas and lifestyles are defended by millions of American teenagers due to the fact that he is one of their gods. He said, "I am bisexual, and I am proud of it. Anything I can do to help the cause I will." (Spin, 10/86, p.91) The most recent album released by *Culture Club* is entitled, *From Luxury to Heartache*. It contains a song entitled, *Sexuality*. Boy George's greatest followers are from the Junior High age group. Think of these young teenagers walking around singing the words to a song called, *Sexuality*. He once said, "I don't believe in God—we all go down into the earth and come back as maggots and that sort of thing." That explains *Culture Club's* song, *Church of the Poison Mind*.

Cinderella - This "Johnny-come-lately" band was first discovered, then promoted by *Bon Jovi* star, Jon Bon Jovi. He not only talked his record company into signing them, but also sang a few back up portions on their debut album, *Night Songs*. At the time of this writing, that album is found in the 'Best Seller' section of most record stores. Like their slightly softer contemporary friend/promoter, *Cinderella* thrives on sex. Perhaps the album does not give the lyrics on the cover or in the sleeve, because they are too vulgar. For one who is not used to it, it is also difficult to catch the words by listening to the album, because the music is so loud and the voices slither and scream around the notes. The few words I was able to understand appalled me. The second song on the first side tells a first person story of a man meeting a girl. She asked him to meet her again and they ended up having sex through the entire night. *"She wrapped her love around me all night long. In the morning we were still going strong. Now let me tell you it felt real good . . . I knew it would. Now let me tell you it felt real right. No poking, teasing and no no fight. She said, 'SHAKE ME, SHAKE ME, SHAKE ME all night long' . . . And now and then she makes those social calls . . . Now let me tell you it felt real tight, and we were shakin' after every bite. I see her comin' in the middle of the night, 'screaming, auhr, auhr, SHAKE ME . . . .'"* The song, *In From the Outside* says, *"Beer by the glass, got a little ass three or four times a day."* Push Push relays another story of the singer's sexual experience. He describes it in explicit terms. *"I'm getting hot, I've got to get a shot. She wants it all, and that's a lot. I'm gettin' long, stiff and steady. I'm gettin' sticky, I thought she couldn't miss me. She looked at me and said, I need a little PUSH PUSH. Got to give a little PUSH PUSH."* Then to take care of any question as to what kind of push this woman was asking for, they change the word 'push' to: *"Can you take a little PUSS PUSS? Then you get a little PUSS PUSS."* The song continues on with like "garbage." What kind of mind will the millions of American teenagers have who daily allow themselves to be mesmerized by this music?

Devo - A few years ago this group was in the top ranks of popularity. They were the group that actually initialized the whip crack beat that became so popular. They did so with the song, *Whip It*, which is street lingo for masturbation. In *Thru Being Cool* they sing: *"We're through being cool. Eliminate the ninnies and the twits. Going to bang some heads, going to beat some butts. Time to show those evil spuds what's what . . . ."* Who are the evil spuds, ninnies and twits? When asked they replied, ". . . the guys in the polyester suits beating Bibles . . . ." (Creem, 1/82, p.43)

The Dead Kennedies - A punk group that is known for its explicit lyrics. The lead singer, Jello Biafra (actual name is Eric Boucher), ran for Mayor of San Francisco in 1979! (Herald—Examiner, Los Angeles, CA, 6/4/86) Biafra along with four others were recently charged with distributing pornographic materials to minors. Included in their third album, *Franchenchrist*, was a 20 by 24 inch poster of 10 close-up male and female genitals engaged in intercourse! What is Biafra's reaction to the charges? "This is a First Amendment, freedom of speech issue. This is a direct result of the nationwide move by right wing and religious organizations to impose via ratings and bannings of rock music and other forms of art and literature." (Times, Los Angeles, CA, 6/4/86) The same picture is too explicit for *Playboy* magazine to print, but this man desires the right to distribute it at will to our children in the name of art. The following is another example of the *Dead Kennedies* wholesome art, it is a song entitled *I Kill Children*: *"I kill children, I love to see them die. I kill children and make their mamas cry. Crush 'em under my car, I wanna hear them scream. Feed 'em poison candy to spoil their Halloween. I kill children, I bang their heads in doors. I kill children, I can hardly* *wait for yours.*" In light of the words to that song, listen to what Biafra said concerning the morals of the band, "Our band stands against exploitation and the glorification of violence." (Times, Los Angeles, CA, 6/4/86) Certainly they do, unless of course it has to do with the murdering of children or the distribution of explicit pornography to minors. They have another song entitled, *Religious Vomit.*

Ded Engine - Many groups today are singing about outright murder, not being against it, but in favor of it and even promoting it. Here is the song entitled, *Blood Lust* by *Ded Engine,* " . . . *Stalk the night, I search for you. Seamy side where the movies are blue . . . Blood lust, I've got blood lust . . . Icy bite, your're growing cold, lost your life, now you've lost your soul. Blood lust . . . I've got blood lust.*"

Def Leppard

Def Leppard - In the video of their hit, *Bringing on the Heartache,* they put their lead singer on a cross, in mockery of the cross of Jesus Christ. Their first album was entitled, *Getcha Rocks Off* (street lingo for an orgasm).

Rick Derringer - His song, *Sweet Evil*, has these lyrics: *"Take me to the bottom, show me where to sell my soul. A promise sealed in blood that says I'm never gonna grow old. It goes on and on, it don't feel so wrong, that sweet evil . . . ."*

Ronnie James Dio - He kicked off in Rock stardom with *Ritchie Blackmore's Rainbow*. With four albums "under his belt", he left and became lead singer for *Black Sabbath* after Ozzy Osbourne had gone solo. Since leaving *Black Sabbath*, his own band has been perhaps more popular than the former. The music, lyrics and videos are filled with occultic themes and symbolism. The word 'Dio' in Spanish means 'god!' Yet, the way Ronnie spells it on his album covers, when it is turned upside down, clearly spells 'Devil.' (Creem-Metal, 10/85, p.8) Incidently, his real name is not Dio. It is Ronnie James Padavana. He simply renamed himself god and spelled it in such a way that it will also spell devil when inverted. By his own admission, he is not just playing games with the occultic themes. He said, "At least I understand something about the occult . . . in order to write logically and sensibly about a subject, you have to learn about it." (Hit Parader, 2/85, p.17) "I'm informed about the darker side of our lives . . . ." (Faces, 2/85, p.17)

I was very disturbed a short time ago upon receiving a telephone call from a concerned father. His elementary school child was given an informative reading sheet that was entitled, *DIO, "We do only one thing—we rock!"* The entire article was written to build up Ronnie James Dio, informing the young reader that he is a worthy star to look up to and admire. In that article geared for young impressionable minds, they say this: "Dio says that his music has nothing to do with witchcraft or devil worship."

(Oh yes? That's not what he said in both *Hit Parader* and *Faces* magazines.) The magazines quote him, "I don't have to explain how stupid I think that is . . . I know how to rock and I know how to create strong images in my songs . . . This whole uproar about rock music and devil worship is nothing more than a bad joke. The only ones who take it seriously are those determined to 'kill' rock and roll." What child wants to be accused of being a "party pooper" trying to kill rock and roll? After all that, in the question section on the back they ask, "Do you think images of witchcraft or devil worship are dangerous in music?"

These poor children have just been told that anybody who thinks such a thing is trying to kill rock and roll. Then the children are supposed to answer this question! This is none other then a mild method of "psychological mind bending" or to put it bluntly, "brainwashing." This is going on right under our noses in the school system that we pay for with our tax dollars! The song *Hungry for Heaven* says, *"You're hungry for heaven but you need a little hell."* One album is entitled, *Holy Diver*. The cover pictures the devil casting a chained clergyman into a lake of fire. He has the face of a goat (occultic symbolism for Satan) and is making the goat's head sign (Devil's Tridad or Il Cornuto) with his hand. Dio is trying to portray his belief that Satan has power over Christianity.

Duran Duran - Just a few months ago, this band was considered to be the most popular band in rock and roll. Only three of the original band members are still together, yet there is little doubt that they will continue to enjoy rock stardom for years to come. The group has a reputation for mystical songs. This "mysticism" has its roots in the occult. One of their "hottest" albums, *Seven*

Duran Duran

and the Ragged Tiger, has a symbol on the backside that can only be found in *The Satanic Bible:* under "The Nine Satanic Statements." Their videos are equally mystical as the songs, filled with astrology symbolism and themes. The video to their hit, *Save a Prayer,* shows the group mesmerizing children and bowing down to an idol. Some song titles include, *The Union of the Snake, New Moon on Monday,* and *New Religion.* The video for *Girls On Film* was banned for being too pornographic.

Eagles - The *Eagles* have never been considered a hard rock group. In fact, they are called by some, "Country Rock." They are the classic illustration to disprove the common idea that occultism in Rock is limited to the hard rock groups or the heavy metal bands. That is a false conception. Few groups exceed the Eagles in occultic activities. Here is a portion of the words to one of their most popular songs, *One of these Nights: "The full moon is calling, the fever is high, and the wicked wind whispers in my ears. You got your demons, you got desires, well I got a few of my own . . . I've been searching for the daughter of the devil himself."* Another of their songs is entitled, *Witchy Woman.* It reads, *"Sparks fly from her*

Eagles

fingertips, echoed voices in the night, she's a restless spirit on an endless flight." Good Day in Hell *says, "In that good book of names, I wanna' go down in flames, seein' how I'm going down . . . Fire, devil's on the phone laughs and says you're doing just fine."* The album *Hotel California,* is considered today to be a classic. The song for which the album is named is very eerie and does not seem to make much sense, until one learns the story behind *Hotel California.* When the First Church of Satan moved into San Francisco, CA, only one property was available to them. It was a hotel on California Street. When one looks closely at the inside of the album cover, he can see the face of Anton Levey, the High Priest of the

Eagles

Satanic Church in San Francisco and the author of *The Satanic Bible*. Larry Salter, the recording manager of the *Eagles*, said that the group had dealings with that church. (Waco Tribune Herald, 2/28/82) Having this information in mind, the song makes a lot more sense. It is clear that they were talking about their church in the song *Hotel California*. They named themselves Eagles after the chief Spirit of the Indian Cosmos. They claim that they wrote most of their songs while under the halucinating drug "Peyote." (Time, 8/15/75, p.4) The group is disbanded but many of their hits, including the above, receive generous air time even today.

Sheena Easton - The words to the song *Sugar Walls* should be considered obscene: *"The blood races to your private spots that lets me know there's a fire. You can't fight, passion is hot, temperatures rise inside my sugar walls. Lem'me take you somewhere you've never been. I could show things you've never seen. I could make you never wanna fall in love again. Come spend the night inside my sugar walls. Take advantage, it's alright. I feel so alive when I'm with you! Come and feel my presence— it's reigning tonight. Heaven on earth inside my sugar walls. I can tell you want me, it's impossible to hide. Your body's on fire. Admit it! Come inside . . . Come spend the night inside my sugar walls."* This song was not an obscure number hidden away on some "behind the counter" album. The album, *A Private Heaven*, was a smash and as a single, *Sugar Walls* went platinum. That means it sold over one million copies, most of these to young girls!

Exodus - The album *Bonded by Blood* contains this song entitled after the name of the band, *Exodus*. *"It starts with life, a way to live, I love the sound of pain. The more it hurts the better I feel . . . It comes to me late at night, when I feel like being cruel, whip out the chains, get the knife and slay some innocent fool . . . The filthy sound of death and pain brings pleasure that I need. The rotting hide, the burning flesh, the smell and I agree. Bloody corpse makes me feel great . . . ."* It is hard to believe that people are able to deny the fact that lyrics like these, coupled with a mesmerizing beat, have a negative effect on those listening. "Negative effect" barely begins to define what rock and roll is doing to its victims.

Fleetwood Mac—Stevie Nicks

Stevie Nicks

Fleetwood Mac—Stevie Nicks - About a decade ago, this group hit stardom with the album, *Rumors*. Earlier albums had been popular but this made the record books by topping the charts for the most consecutive weeks. Several of the album's singles also were number one on the singles billboard. It is interesting to note that all the music was published by the *Welsh Witch Publishing Company*. This is not a fictitious name. Much of the occultic material that enters into our country is published by the Welsh Witch Publishing Company. In fact, they had a song entitled, *Rhianon*, which is about a "welsh witch." Stevie Nicks' (since popular *"Fleetwood Mac"* days she has been a hit with her own recordings) song, *Lonely Night*, was dedicated to all the lonely witches in the world. She posed as a witch on some of her solo album covers. On the cover of *Bella Donna* she claims to be posing as a white witch. Anton Levey says, "Call it black, call it white, call it what you will. It's all evil, and it all gets its power from the source of hell." *Bella Donna* is a plant from which witches claim they obtain the most powerful ingredients for potions. Stevie Nicks is not just playing a game. *Rolling Stone* says that she is openly involved with the occult. Stevie Nicks is serious about what she is doing.

Samantha Fox - This new female rocker is attempting to emerge as another of Rock's sex symbols. Her new increasingly popular album features a picture of herself with a large tear in the back of her faded blue jeans exposing a bare backside. The album title (which I am sure is deliberately captioned for the picture) is *Touch Me*. The songs on the LP are full of the same topic. One title is, *He's got Sex*.

Frankie Goes to Hollywood - The album *Welcome to the Pleasure Dome* has this quote in it, "Manipulation of children's minds in the field of religion or politics would touch off a parental storm and a rash of congressional investigations. But in the world of commerce, children are fair game and legitimate prey."

Grateful Dead - This band was originally known as the "Warlocks" (male witches). Jerry Garcia, spokesman for the group said, "Acid rock is music you listen to when you are high on acid." (Rolling Stone, 2/3/72, p.30) Robert

Hunter, who writes most of the lyrics for the group, said this in his *Ten Commandments of Rock and Roll*, "Destroy yourself physically and mentally and insist that all true brothers do likewise as an act of unity." Evidently his "brother band member" Don (pigpen) McKernan went along with his insistings and died as a result of drug abuse.

Grim Reaper

Grim Reaper - The Grim Reaper is a tarot card (occultic fortune telling card) figure that is the devil's "angel of death." This group's first album was entitled, *See You in Hell*. Some titles of songs include, *Dead on Arrival* and *Wrath of the Reaper*. The album covers are filled with themes of death, the Grim Reaper and hellfire.

Daryl Hall - Together with John Oates he made up the previously popular Hall -n- Oates. He is an admitted homosexual. "The idea of sex with a man doesn't turn me off." (Rolling Stone, 4/21/77, p.15) The video to *Adult Education* is clearly occultic. He is a follower of *Aleister Crowley*, the leading Satanist during the early part of this century. He also admits to the practicing of magic. (Circus, 10/13/77, p.28) (Sixteen, 5/81, p.26) Maybe that is where he got the idea for the title of the song, *Possession Obsession*.

Daryl Hall

Debra Harry - This one time "Blondie" star now going solo is an ex-*Playboy* bunny. She said, "I've always thought that the main ingredients in Rock are . . . sex and sass." (Hit Parader, 9/79, p.31) Earlier she had said, "Rock and Roll is all sex, 100%." (Circus, 7/7/77, p.40) Her live-in lover/manager, Chris Stein, seemed to agree with her. He said, "Everyone takes it for granted that Rock and Roll is synonymous with sex." (People, 5/21/79) She has a song entitled, *Die Young and Stay Pretty*. In that song she sings, *"Don't get old and ugly, die young and stay pretty."* The song encourages suicide in a day when

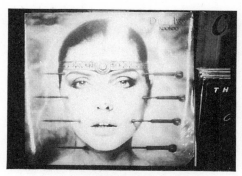

Debra Harry

teenage suicide is up over 200%. For some time, Debra was "back in the woodwork" (reportedly nursing Chris Stein back to health) until her late single, *French Kissin'* and brand new album, *Rockbird* were recently released.

Heart - Ann and Nancy Wilson have for years been reported to have been involved with the occult. One of their hits is a song entitled, *Devil Delight*. The words go like this: *"You might feel me burning all night, like a dirty demon daughter, don't put up no fight, I'll dance in the spotlight, I'm all right, it's just my devil, my devil's delight."*

Heart

Billy Idol

Billy Idol - His video, *Eyes Without a Face*, shows an idol in a flaming Satanist circle with a hooded figure in the background. He has an album entitled, *Flesh for Fantasy*. Not long ago when Idol was in Seattle, he was interviewed on radio station, *KISW*, on Gary Crow's afternoon show. Billy's vulgarity was so radical that the station cut him short. He used graphic detail on the air in describing female anatomy and sexual intercourse.

Iron Maiden

Iron Maiden - Shortly after *Iron Maiden* released their *Powerslave* album, people were asking questions as to why they used such a strong Egyptian theme on the album and the tour. It was learned that the album was filled with Egyptian occultic symbolism. They were starting to get some bad press over it. About that time, Bruce Dickenson started coming out on stage during concert and making the announcement that certain rumors were not true and that the Egyptian theme was just for fun. However, shortly before this time he told *Hit Parader*, "The Egyptian idea came because of my interest in religion and magic and all that weird stuff . . . The idea of *Powerslave* is to get enough magic on the album that it'd rub off on the whole event." (Hit Parader, 4/85, p.4) Bass Steve Harris said that occultic things fascinate the band. (Creem, 9/82, p.44) Understand, "lying" is not taboo in the Satanic church. A little later Dickenson said, ". . . we've referred to things like the tarot (occultic fortune telling cards) and ideas of people like Aleister Crowley." (Circus, 8/31/84) Aleister Crowley, as you remember, is the famous Satanist. During one tour, the band opened up concerts with the words, *"Welcome to Satan's Sanctuary."* Iron Maiden also has an album entitled, *Number of the Beast.* The number of the beast of course is 666 and is explained in the book of *Revelation.* Who else beside a Christian would know of such things? Those who are ardently involved with the opposing religion, namely occultism. Also, on the backside of that album, *Revelation 13:18* is misquoted. All of their album covers picture either demonic creatures or occultic references of some sort. Songs include, *Purgatory, Prodigal Son, Number of the Reaper, Hallowed be Thy Name* and *Charlotte the Harlot.* Here are the words to *The Number of the Beast*: *"In the night the fires burning bright, the ritual has begun, Satan's work is done . . . Sacrifice is going tonight . . . I feel drawn toward the evil chanting hordes. They seem to mesmerize me, can't avoid their eyes. 666, the number of the beast. 666, the one for you and me. I'm coming back, I will return and possess your body . . . ."* Charlotte the Harlot *is not the only song they have about prostitution. These are part of the lyrics to* 22 Acacia Ave.*, a song about another prostitute: ". . . Beat her, mistreat her, do anything you please. Bite her, excite her, make her get down on her knees. Abuse her, misuse her, she can take all you got. Caress her, molest her, she always does what you want."*

Michael Jackson

Michael Jackson - Michael Jackson has been hailed as being the good boy on the rock scene. He seems to be such a nice, well mannered young man. America will probably never know how extent the damages are that Michael Jackson has brought upon her young people— not until eternity. Many of his popular songs contain illicit sex such as *Billie Jean* and *The Lady in my Life*. In *Body* he sings, *"Girl I want your body! Girl I need your body! Girl I want your body! won't you come home with me?"* Beside the sex, Michael Jackson is a *Jehovah's Witness*. He gives millions of dollars to this group. The next time you buy a Michael Jackson T-shirt, or baseball cap, or album, know that you may well be making a contribution to the Jehovah's Witnesses. There is said to be evidence that Michael Jackson is involved in the occult. His earlier hit, *Beat It* contains backmasking with the words, *"Believe in Satan."* The video, *Thriller*, the all time "most popular" video, cost millions to produce. It so "reeked" in occultic themes that for fear of bad press, Jackson made a statement at the onset of the video to say that due to his strong convictions, he did not believe in the occult. Yet in the song he sings, *"There are demons closing in on every side, they will possess you!"* He also included Vincent Price in the video to cast a spell on those that are listening. Vincent Price by the way is not only an "actor." He is also a self-proclaimed warlock and has a book out on "spellcasting!" All this from Michael Jackson, an "innocent" boy of rock and roll.

Billy Joel

Billy Joel - In his song, *Only the Good Die Young*, Billy Joel remorses over the fact that religious girls stay virgins so long. He goes on to sing, *"Some say there's a heaven, I say there ain't. I'd rather laugh with the sinners than cry with the saints, sinners have much more fun."*

Elton John - It would be easy to write an entire chapter on this man. However, due to the dying popularity of his music and limited space in this book, we will not. During the "seventies", this rocker was a megastar. Yet, to say the least, both his lifestyle and songs were vile. *All the Girls Love Alice* is about a lesbian. It was songs like these that helped pave and seal the way for the "gay rights" movement. Elton John is an admitted homosexual and he exploits it with his songs. *"There's nothing wrong with going to bed with somebody of your own sex. I just think people should be very free with sex."* (Rolling Stone, 10/7/76, p.17) It is amazing to see how many of those who have such loose morals are associated with the occult. Bernie Taupin, Elton John's partner and former co-writer said this, "Elton John's home is laden with trinkets and books relating to Satanism and witchcraft." Satan's ultimate goal is to get people in hell to spend eternity in misery with him. What greater way to reach the goal of "suicide" than to prey upon people who have not received Christ as Savior? Listen to the lyrics of this Elton John song: *I'm getting bored being part of mankind. There's not a lot to do no more, this race is a waste of time . . . Yeah, think I'm gonna kill myself, cause a little suicide. Stick around for a couple of days, what a scandal if I die. Yeah, I'm gonna kill myself, cause a little headline news. Like to see what the papers say on the state of the teenage blues."*

Judas Priest - The name of this group sounds blasphemous but it seems "tame" compared to Rob Halfor's original band named *"Lord Lucifer."* The song and album titles are equally occultic with songs like *The Devil's Child* and albums such as *Sin after Sin* and *Defenders of the Faith.* When asked the meaning of the title of the latter album, Halfor answered, "We're defending the faith of

Judas Priest

heavy metal music." (Hit Parader, 5/84, p.16) Words to
The Devil's Child go like this: *"Oh, no, you're so d___ed
wicked. You got me by the throat . . . You never let
me go . . . I gave my body as a slave. You cut my flesh
and drank my blood that poured in streams . . . ."* Several
of their songs contain backmasked messages. *Some Heads
are Gonna Roll* has the backwards message, *"Oh, the
Lord is headless." Love Bites* says, *"I love violence."* They
also glorify sexual themes. *Defenders of the Faith* contains
the song *Eat Me Alive* which has these appalling words,
*"Squealing in passion as the rod of steel injects, gut
wrenching frenzy that deranges every joint, I'm gonna
force you at gun point to eat me alive."*

Keel - Their album, *The Right to Rock,* produced by
Kiss's Gene Simmons, has a blasphemous portrayal of
the Ark of the Covenant found in *Exodus 25.*

KISS - I have been ridiculed for making the statement
that *KISS* stands for *Kids in Satan's Service.* People tell
me, "Oh, that was made up by some preacher, *KISS* denies
they even had that in mind!" Well I have it in black and
white, you can look it up for yourself, and by the way,

KISS

it's a secular periodical—*American Photographer*, January of 1980, page 6. The ex-drummer for the group, Peter Criss, once said, "I find myself evil. I believe in the devil as much as I believe in God. You can use either one to get things done." (Rolling Stone, 7/7/77, p.49) What's he talking about? Probably the same thing as *Black Sabbath* when they named an album *We Sold Our Soul for Rock and Roll*. Gene Simmons, one of the original members and who seems to be the spokesman for the group said, "If God is such hot stuff then why is he afraid to have other gods before Him? . . . I guess I always wanted to be God, there's nothing higher than God." (Circus, 9/13/76, p.42) According to some who are aquainted with cannibalism, it is part of occultic worship associated with demonism in tribal nations and Satanism even here in America. Gene Simmons goes through antics on stage that are closely associated with cannibalistic practices. He once said this, "I've always wondered what human flesh tastes like and I've always wanted to be a cannibal." (Circus, 9/13/76, p.42) Paul Stanley said this in an interview, *"You know what we've been getting a lot of lately? . . . Letters from sixteen and seventeen year olds with little polaroid pictures of them naked.*

That's amazing. That's great. There's nothing like knowing you're helping the youth of America." (Circus, 1/20/76, p.36) That statement matches many of their songs well. Here is _Fits Like a Glove_ off the _Lick It Up_ LP: _"Ain't a cardinal sin, Baby, let me in . . . Girl I'm gonna treat you right . . . Well goodness sakes my snakes alive and its ready to bite . . . Baby let me in . . . Fits like a glove . . . Think I'm gonna burst. When I go through her . . . It's like a hot knife through butter."_ The same album contains this song: _"Hot Blood, need your love. Hard as Rock, can't get enough. Wanna feel you deep inside, pumpin' through my veins . . . Fill you to the core . . . Like a dog to the bone, make you sweat, make you moan . . . Come on lick my candy cane . . . ."_ The song, _God of Thunder_ reads like this, _"I was raised by demons . . . I'm the Lord of the wasteland. I gather darkness to please me. I command you to kneel before the god of thunder, the god of rock and roll. The spell you're under will slowly rob you of your virgin soul . . . ."_ As if his music wasn't having a big enough influence on teenagers, listen to Gene Simmons advice to the youth of America: _"Survival's gotta do with believing in yourself, period. People are going to tell you, 'You can't do this. You can't do that.' They can all go f___ themselves collectively . . . You don't need them around, and that includes your parents . . . Get rid of those leeches and go after your dreams."_ (Faces, 12/84)

Krokus - This is an upcoming group now gaining popularity. The album, _Alive and Screaming_ features a demonic figure. _Headhunter_ portrays a giant skull and crossbones. Remember the reoccurring theme of death is also present in the occult. All of their album covers contain the Satanic 'S' (dealt with in the next section) that is shared with the likes of _KISS, Black Sabbath,_

AC/DC and others. Songs include: *Eat the Rich, Screaming in the Night,* and *Ready to Burn. Out to Lunch* says, *"Got a beat up Cadillac . . . Slippin' out now I won't be back. There's a party down the road . . . Got a girl, gonna take my load . . . Give it to me all night long. Let it in 'till the break of dawn . . . ."*

Cyndi Lauper

Cyndi Lauper - Talking about the three major institutions in America: the church, the family and the state, she said, *"You know what I learned? Those are the three biggest oppressors of women that will ever come along."* (Newsweek, 3/4/85, p.50) Little does she know that there has never been a more exaggerated oppression of women's rights and integrity than what is being done through pornography. And Cyndi is a large part of that industry with her music! Her song, *She Bop* is a celebration of masterbation. *All Through the Night* is as filthy as the title hints.

Led Zeppelin - Although since the death of drummer John Bonham this group is no longer together, they nevertheless are considered to be a legend. Hundreds of groups attempt to capture the sound that *Led Zeppelin* made famous. The interior of their *Stairway to Heaven* album cover has an enlarged picture of the tarot card figure "The Hermit." The album, *Houses of the Holy* pictures naked girls climbing up an ancient Babylonian ziggurat. On the inside is a picture of a priest dressed in occultic garb holding one of these (dead) girls up to a strange light. It appears as though the girl was sacrificed to this occultic deity. Robert Plant, who has since gone "solo", said that he had a fascination for black magic but Jimmy Page, now with *The Firm*, has an obsession for it. Jimmy Page, until recently, owned one of the largest occultic bookstores in London. It is called "Equinox" (also the title of one of Styx's albums). (Creem, 11/79) *Aleister Crowley is a name that is synonymous with the occult.* During the early part of this century, he was the leading Satanist in the world. He owned huge mansions both in Italy (until expelled for practicing human sacrifice with newborn babies) and Scotland which he used for his occultic practices. Jimmy Page bought the mansion in Scotland and has written songs in it, including *Stairway to Heaven* (now claimed to be one of the all time most popular songs). In April of 1982 the CBS Evening News revealed the fact that when played backwards, the song contains many Satanic quotations. About that song, Page said, "Somebody else pushed the pen." Page's new group isn't much better. Here is one of their hits entitled, *Radioactive*: "*I want to stay with you, I want to play with you, I want to lay with you, and I want you to know, got to concentrate, don't be distractive, turn me on tonight, 'cause I'm radioactive.*"

Huey Lewis and the News - This San Francisco-based band first hit the limelight with the multiplatinum album, *SPORTS*. The LP contained a top ten hit entitled, *I Want a New Drug*. Although the song is not about narcotics,

Huey Lewis and the News

there is no doubt as to what the connotations are. The opening song on their latest album, *FORE!*, is *Jacob's Ladder*. The song is a slap at Christianity, making fun of a *". . . fat man selling salvation in his hand . . . ."* The second verse says, *"Comin' over the airwaves, the man says I'm overdue. Sing along, send some money, join the chosen few. Hey mister, I'm not in a hurry, and I don't want to be like you . . . ."* Huey Lewis and the News are also good at infiltrating their songs with sex. The fairly recent, *Whole Lotta Lovin'* is about a man who is reading pornographic magazines. He says he's tired of that and instead of dreaming he would like to get back to the real thing. In *I Know What I Like*, he tells young people, *"I don't like no one to tell me what to do."*

Live Skull - Here is just a sample of their "wholesome" music, *"You know I'm coming to wreck your life, to tear your face off, and drive a stake through the heart of your loved one . . . ."*

Lizzy Borden - This song, *Flesh Eater*, is on their album, *Love You to Pieces: "I growl for my meat while you bark for the bone. I plunge in so deep, you swallow me whole.*

You lust for my tongue, it makes me feel mean, I bound your arms and lick you clean. You scream with delight as you frantically fight . . . Flesh eater, she wants it deeper, flesh eater, I want to eat her."

Madonna

Madonna - *"A lot of what I am about is just expressing sexual desire and not caring what people think about it."* (Time, 5/27/85, p.81) She has been called names such as "Bimbo" and "Slut", but what is her reaction to such criticism? *"As long as I'm riding high on the charts, I don't care what they call me. I like my trashy image."* In the smash album and single, *Like a Virgin*, she sang of being *"touched for the very first time"*. Then she sings, *"Feels so good inside . . . ."* Something to remember about Madonna; today as being the most popular female vocalist ever, she draws mostly from early teen and pre-teen girl audiences. Little girls idolize the woman. If there is one question in the minds of girls in this age group it is, "How can I be accepted by my peers and especially boys?" The millions of teenage girls who follow Madonna are sadly led astray! Her latest album, *True Blue*, contains a song that was a hit entitled, *Papa Don't Preach*. It is a song about a teenage girl that gets pregnant out of wedlock. She tells her father not to preach and that no matter what he says, she's going to keep her baby. In the video, at the end of the song, the father and the girl hug and all seems well. The message is clear. In the song, all turns out for the better. The boy is going to marry her and she winds up with a better relationship with her father. The girl seems better off having gotten pregnant than before. If that doesn't get a young girl, who is afraid of losing her boyfriend and is having problems with her parents (millions of them just like that around this country), to consider joining our nation's epidemic of teenage pregnancies, what will? Madonna appears nude in the motion picture, *A Certain Sacrifice*. The movie is full of sex and violence (including Madonna getting raped) plus occultic references with a human sacrifice as a climax. In, *Crazy for You* (from the movie, *Vision Quest*) she sings, *"Strangers makin' the most of the dark. Two by two their bodies become one."* On stage and in pictures, Madonna usually has either a cross, often times many crosses, or a crucifix hanging around her neck or from her ears. During an interview with *Time* magazine she was asked why. Her answer was, she thinks they're funny. (Time, 5/27/85, p.83) Shortly afterward she was asked why the crucifixes. Listen to her answer, *"Crucifixes are sexy because there is a naked man on them."* (Spin, 5/85)

Malsteen - The album, *Marching Out* contains the song, *Disciples of Hell*. Here are a portion of the words: *"In the darkness they will gather, conjuring the one. Burning candles, incantations, human sacrifice. Getting drunk from blood not wine, pointing daggers shine. Out of fire, smoke, and brimstone the dreaded one will rise! Nobody knows who's disciples of hell, bother the priest and he's casting a spell. No one can stop what's already begun. Worshipping darkness and Lucifer's son!"*

Mary Jane Girls - This is a new upcoming group that has just started to gain stardom. How are they doing it? *Song Hits Yearbook* tells us: "While enticing legions of hotblooded males with their unadulterated and uncensored lyrics and sultry vocals, this funky foursome have also captured a loyal female following with their honesty and push for sexual freedom. Songs of sex, love and more sex fill their *Only Four You* album from the opening groove to the last." (Song Hits Yearbook, Fall 1986, p.32) Here is just a mild sample of what that article is talking about with their much requested hit, *Wild and Crazy Love.* *"Baby you've got a sexy body, I think I ought to tell you so. You look so deep and so delicious, I kiss you from your head to toe. If there's a chance I could romance you. I'd make you scream in sheer delight. I'd give you so much love and pleasure, you'd want to make love every night . . . Now tonight's the night for love, I'm gonna give my all to you. Wild and crazy love. I'm gonna have a ball with you . . . I'm gonna give it to you . . . You set a fire through my body, whenever I make love to you . . . But as for now, when you want me, just open up and come on in . . . ."*

John McLaughlin - This man has been known to have his audience join him in meditation while in concert. He said this, *"One night we were playing and suddenly the spirit entered into me, and I was playing, but it was no longer me playing."* That is a phenomenon that many rock guitarists have described.

Meatloaf - John Steinman of the group said, *"I've always been fascinated by the supernatural and always felt rock was the perfect idiom for it."* (Circus, 12/22/77, p.12) He also said in *Time* magazine that when he gets on stage, he gets possessed. (Time, 9/11/78)

Megadeath - This band will be heard of more in the future. They recently signed a six album contract with *Capital Records* and are now on their way. (Evening Observer, Dunkirk, NY, 10/30/86) Their first album describes the character of the band, *Killing is Our Business.* The band's figurehead is the skull of a torture victim named *VIC.* The latest of their releases is entitled, *'Peace Sells but Who's Buying?'*

John Cougar Mellencamp

John Cougar Mellencamp - Mellencamp tries to maintain a Springsteen type working class image. He sings of middle class problems, farm communities, etc. Also like Springsteen, he is far from innocent. He once said, ". . . I hate schools, governments and churches." (People, 10/82) Beside the blatant sex in songs such as, *Hurt So Good* and *I Need a Lover,* Mellencamp enjoys poking fun at Christianity. In *Golden Gates* he sings, *"I don't need to see a woman crying for the Savior, holding onto some money-man's hand. Who can I call to make reservations forever thrown in the dark."* In *Serious Business* he sings, *'This is serious business; sex, violence and rock and roll . . . take my life, take my soul, put me on the cross for all to see. Put my name around my neck, let those people throw stones at me. This is serious business; sex, drugs, violence and rock and roll."*

Mentors - Just a few of the despicable songs by this group are, *Free Fix for a F___, My Erection is Over,* and *Golden Showers.* The lyrics to the latter song are as follows: *"Listen little slut, do as you are told. Come with daddy for me to pour the gold. All through my excrements you shall roam, Open your mouth and taste the foam."*

Mercyful Fate - The album, *Don't Break the Oath* is hard to believe. This group is a genuine, pull out all the stops, Satanic worshipping rock band. They don't "beat around the bush." They "claim" to be and "prove" to be in league with Lucifer. The following word are printed on the inside sleeve of the album: *"By the symbol of the Creator, I swear henceforth to be a faithful servant of his most puissant arch-angel, the prince Lucifer, whom the Creator designated as His regent and lord of this world. Amen. I deny Jesus Christ, the deceiver, and I abjure the Christian Faith, holding in contempt all of its works. As a being now possessed of a human body in this world, I swear to give my full allegiance to its lawful master, to worship him, our lord Satan, and no other. In the name of Satan, the ruler of Earth. Open wide the gates of hell and come forth from the abyss by these names: Satan, Leviathan, Belial, Lucifer. I will kiss the goat. I will swear to give my mind, my body and soul, unreservedly, to the furtherance of our lord Satan's designs. Do what thou wilt, shall be the whole of the law. As it was in the beginning, is now, and ever shall be, world without end, Amen."* It is heart breaking to imagine it, but think of the thousands of teenagers who bought that album, took it home, then recited the words on the sleeve and sang the song.

Metallica - Many of their songs are eerie, mystical and occultic. According to *Circus* magazine, Kirk Hammet of the band is a follower of a man named H. P. Lovecraft. (As was their bass, now deceased Cliff Burton.) Lovecraft was a writer during the early part of this century who dwelt on occultic themes. Cliff also was a proponent of a fantasy projection game like *Dungeons and Dragons* adapted from the Lovecraft epic, *The Call of Cthulhu.* Suicide is a common theme both in rock and the occult. Their song, *Fade to Black* is about suicide. In fact, they sing of desiring it. Their album was entitled, *Kill 'Em All.*

Molly Hatchet - This band got their name from a seventeenth century Salem woman who beheaded her lovers with an axe. (Rock 'n' Roll and the Occult, Harrisburg, PA)

Motley Crue

Motley Crue - This group makes no apology for their Satanism. The cover of the album, *Shout at the Devil,* closely resembles the cover of the Satanic Bible. A portion of the words to *Bastard* say, *"Out go the lights, in goes my knife, pull out his life, consider that bastard dead."* The most innocent title on the album is, *Too Young to Fall in Love.* However, the words are far from innocent. *"Not a woman but a whore, I can taste the hate. Well*

Motley Crue

now I'm killing you, watch your face turning blue." On the cover of the album are the words, "This record may contain backward masking." It does. At one point on the album are the words, *"Backward mask where you are, oh, lost in error, Satan."* It is interesting to note that blatant Satanism and blatant sex go hand in hand. On the same album is a song entitled, *Ten Seconds to Love.* The song is about quick sex on an elevator. The words are unbelievably disgusting; *"Touch my gun but don't pull the trigger, shine my pistol some more, here I come . . . reach down low, slide it in real slow . . . you feel so good, do you want some more? I got one more shot, my gun's still warm."* Their most recent album is entitled, *Theatre of Pain.* The record contains the song, *We Need a Lover Tonight.* It is actually an appeal for a girl to sexually satisfy them all night after a concert. Here are the vile words, *"90,000 screaming watts, honey dripping from her pot. Pleasure victim, who's next to fall? . . . The question is can you please us all tonight? . . . Slide down my knees and taste my sword. Can you feel the power inside tonight?*

We need a lover tonight." In Albuquerque, New Mexico, Vince Neil shouted to a screaming crowd made up largely of young girls: "There's so much good pussy in Albuquerque! The only thing wrong is that I can't eat it all tonight! (Hit Parader)

Ted Nugent - This fella has been lingering around for quite some time on the hard rock scene. He has a history of violent, drug related and explicitly sexual song material. The album, *Penetrator* contains the song, *Thunder Thighs.* Ted sings, *"She sets me free when she sits on me . . . ."* Talking about his reasons for why he does what he does he said, "I'm in it for the pussy." (Hit Parader, 4/84, p.8) "That's how I know my music is going . . . if the pussy hunting's good, I know I've done a good day's work. I like L.A. because the pussy out there is young and clean . . . ." (Hit Parader, 4/84, p.25)

Nasty Savage - Sado-masochism is another predominant theme in rock and roll today. In fact, that is where the studs, handcuffs, leather and chains on the costumes come from. This band has a song entitled, *Dungeon of Pleasure.* Here are a portion of the words: *". . . Forbidden techniques, it's just what they seek. Fantasy lane, dominance, submission, handcuffs and chains. Bondage and pain . . . The bitch is bound and helpless, she's screaming for more. That sweet and innocent girl is really hard core. Her obsession with pain makes me bite my lip, as she eagerly indulges when I give her the whip."*

Ozzy Osbourne - Until 1980 Ozzy Osbourne was the lead singer for the group *Black Sabbath.* He gave the group much of their occultic flavor. Today, he is more popular then ever and probably more wicked then ever. He once said, "I don't know if I'm a medium for some

Ozzy Osbourne

outside source. Whatever it is, frankly, I hope it's not what I think . . . Satan." (Hit Parader, 2/75, p.24) In 1986, when Ozzy toured in the Los Angeles area, the *Times* reported that paramedics and officials from the local hospitals were swamped with emergency calls that came as a result of Ozzy's concerts . . . emergency calls that included death! (Times, 6/16/86) Inspiring death is not new for Ozzy Osbourne. In 1984, a teenager was found having shot himself in the head with his father's pistol! Still on his head were the headphones from his listening to Ozzy's song, *Suicide Solution*. The song *Paranoid* was also cited in the case as having encouraged the boy toward suicide. It is definitely a suicidal song. ". . . *Oh, won't you blow my brains, Oh yeah! . . . and so as you hear these words, that in you now, if I state, I tell you to end your life. I wish I could mine . . . .*" (UPI, 1/14/86) Talking about Aleister Crowley, he remarked, "That man was the phenomenon of his time." (Circus, 8/26/80) He went so far as to release a song about the man. He once said that he was driven to see the movie, *Exorcist*, 26 times. (Circus, 10/31/75, p.67, 68) His album covers are full of symbolism, which we will see in the next section. His latest album, *The Ultimate Sin*, pictures the book of *Revelation* on the cover. Another album is entitled, *Diary of a Madman*. The song of the same name is about demon possession. A recent horror comedy film entitled, *Trick or Treat*, has Ozzy playing the tongue in cheek role of a religious crusader against rock music on a TV talk show. (Heavy Metal Hotsheets, 11/86, p.19) Ironic to that movie is his song, *"You can't kill rock & roll, cause rock and roll is my religion . . . . "*

John Parr - Many people say, "But the bad songs aren't played on the radio." We beg to differ with you. The following song is a John Parr hit and was listed as one of the top sellers of 1985. (Top Hits of 1985, Hal Leonard Publishing Corp.) The song is entitled, *Naughty Naughty*, and is about the singer talking a girl (evidently a virgin) into having sex with him. *"I put my hand on your stocking, I was moving nice and slow. Let my fingers do the walking and there ain't far to go. Don't tell me, 'I don't want to be a girl like that'. Do you want to see a grown man cry? You don't want to be a girl like that. Baby this could be the first time. (This could be the first time.) . . . Bedroom eyes, they undress me, cut me to the bone. Lace and satin pressed against me, should we call a chaperone . . . Naughty, naughty, cute and horny, t-t-t-t-tease me, Take it easy . . . I'm a naughty, naughty guy . . . With your hair hung down and your dress riding high, and your eyes burning hot like the sun. Kiss me hard, squeeze me tight, wanna love you all night, 'cause I'm a naughty, naughty guy . . . ."* On and on the trash continues.

Pink Floyd - One smash hit by this group has children repeating these words after the group sang them, *"We don't need no education, we don't need no mind control . . . ."* Then the children shout out in unison, *"Hey teachers, leave us kids alone!"* Who is attempting the mind control?

The album, *Animals* contains the song, *Sheep*. Buried in the right channel of the mix, barely audible except by the subconscience, can be heard an eerie voice giving these words: *"The Lord is my shepherd, I shall not want, He maketh me to lie down through pastures green. He leadeth me the silent waters by; with bright knives he releaseth my soul. He makes me to hang on hooks in high places. He converteth me to lamb cutlets. For Lo, he hath great power and great hunger. When cometh the day we lowly ones through quiet reflection and great dedication master the art of karte, we shall raise up and then we shall make the bugger's eyes water."* I never had a teacher put anti-Christian subliminal messages into one of my classes. Still people say, "But this kind of thing has no effect on young people. It's just music." A few years ago, 16 year old Bruce put in the *Pink Floyd* tape, *Good By Cruel World* and killed himself while listening to it. (Gazette-Telegraph, Colorado Springs, CO, 4/23/86) It does have an effect—a devastating one!

Plasmatics - Wendy O. Williams, the famed screamer for the group is noted for her posing half nude on their album covers. At times, she posed and appeared in concert wearing nothing over her breasts but thin strips of black tape or dobs of shaving cream. She was arrested in both Milwaukee and Cleveland for masturbating on stage during concert! Wendy said this some time ago, "We do a real show. And we like to make noise. Every time we play, I have orgasms—specially on *Butcher Baby* . . . I consider us the ultimate American experience. A normal sex act takes a half hour. In a half hour, we do ten songs." (Us magazine, 12/9/80, p.58) Many of their songs and album covers dabble into the occult. They have a song entitled, *Incantation*. Another number, *Doom Song*, is an actual witch's incantation. It ends with these words, *"I command* *that these things of which I speak Will come to be. Behold the Prince of Darkness here!"*

Poison

Poison - This is another new upcoming group that has gained enormous popularity with their latest album. The album, *Look What the Cat Dragged In* pictures all the members of the group with full makeup on. All four of them are males, though they are made up to pass as and could pass as attractive females! Songs contain quite a bit of reference to sex. Titles include: *Play Dirty, Talk Dirty to Me, Want Some Need Some,* and *Number One Bad Boy.*

Police

Police - Led by lead singer "Sting", *Police* first gained popularity when they released a single in Britain. Banned in Britain, they brought it to America where it quickly rose to near the top of the charts. The song's title was, *Roxanne*. Britain banned it because Roxanne was a prostitute. America, however, hailed it as a hit. From that time until now, the Police have been superstars. *Roxanne* was mild compared to some of their later songs. *Murder by Numbers* says: *"You can bump off every member of your family and anyone else you find a bore."* *Can't Stand Losing You* is about suicide. *Be My Girl Sally* is about a rubber sex doll. Another song is entitled, *Bed's Too Big Without You. Set them Free,* according to Sting, came out of his anti-permanent relationships belief. (Musician, 2/87, p.42) In the same article he said this, "When a truly great musician plays, it's almost a sexual thing . . . ." Many of their songs are mystical, such as *Mosoko Tango,* which was inspired by John Blockson, a professor of paraphysics. The album, *Ghost in the Machine,* is very mystical, containing the songs: *Spirits in a Material World, Every Little Bit She Does is Magic, Secret Journey,* and *Darkness.* It is important to note that mysticism walks hand in hand with the occult. The one is never independent of the other. In Sting's own words, "The pure essence of music is very spiritual . . . ." (Musician, 2/87, p.41)

Iggy Pop - This man is one of the forerunners of today's Heavy Metal bands. He began with the group *The Stooges.* Iggy is still around and has his own cult following. He may very will be best remembered for his highly publicized drug problem. This is how he claimed to prepare himself for concerts: "Two grams of biker speed, five trips of LSD and as much grass as could be inhaled before a gig." (Creem, 11/79, p.30) He once turned himself in to an insane asylum. He is noted for deeds in concert such as rolling

around barebacked on broken glass, jumping off stage
into the screaming crowd, and dropping his pants before
audiences and photographers. Iggy said, "I am totally into
corruption." (Creem, 11/79, p.27) Mr. Pop has a particular
disdain for women. He once remarked, "Well, I hate
women. Why do I even have to have a reason for that?
It's like, why are people reviled by insects?" (Creem, 11/79,
p.30) Maybe that's why he sang, *"I got to hit my baby
on a Saturday night."* In the same song (*Loco Mosquito*)
he sings, *"I'm sick of hanging round with old tranvestites.
They stare at my rubbers, it makes me feel uptight."*

Prince

Prince - Detroit, November 4, 1984, as quoted by *Rolling
Stone* (1/17/85, p.33): "He stripped and climbed into a
bathtub. He pounded his pelvis into the floor time and
time again." The article went on to say that he stroked
the neck of his guitar until a fluid shot out the end. His
song, *Sister,* is about his incestial relationship with his
own sister. *"My sister never made love with anyone but
me. Incest is everything it's said to be . . . Motherf___er
can't you understand?"* His song, *Motown*, is about
homosexuality. *Head* is about oral sex. (New Sounds, 1/84,
p.20) *Rolling Stone* magazine said this about his music,

". . . The major tunes are paens to bi-sexuality, incest and cunnilingal technique (having to do with oral sex) . . . at it's best, *Dirty Mind* (album title) is positively filthy." The album, *Purple Rain*, sold over nine million copies! It contains the song, *Darling Nikki*. Who is she? Prince tells us, *"I guess you could say she was a sex fiend. I met her in a motel lobby masturbating with a magazine . . . ."* This magazine quote tells of what a Prince concert consists of, "The blasphemous portion of the show came when after leading the crowd through a Sunday School hymn . . . our anti-hero went through a Jekyll-and-Hyde bit at the keyboard, became possessed by devilish sexual temptation and asked God if He'd like to take a bath with him. At which point he ascended a staircase, stripped to his caballero pants, slid into his tub for a neon green shower . . . ." (Record, 1/85) Much of this trash is being sold to pre-teens. Prince's hit single, *Let's Go Crazy*, had the word "f. .k" on the B side, *Erotic City*, fourteen times. And that song was sold along with the teenybopper hit! It also got quite a bit of air play on the radio. Little 13 year old Alice said this, "Every girl who's seen the movie (referring to Prince's *Purple Rain*) thinks Prince is IT. I mean, he's almost as sexy as Richard Gere . . . He seems in control. That's what's cool. It doesn't make any difference that he's black. And I don't think the songs are dirty, really. I mean they are—but mostly they just show more of what I said. Like he knows what he's doing. Sure I'd like to spend the night with him." (Rock and Roll Confidential Report, Dave Marsh, p.156) The *Los Angeles Herald-Examiner* tells of a 17 year old boy that was obsessed with Prince. He looked like him, and called himself "The Kid" (the name of the character Prince played in the motion picture *Purple Rain*). He was found one early morning having hung himself from a tree in the yard of an elementary school. The headlines read, "SAD

ENDING TO PURPLE RAIN: DESPONDENT BOY CALLED "THE KID" HANGS HIMSELF FROM TREE." (Herald-Examiner, Los Angeles, CA, 6/13/86)

Queen

Queen - "I like strippers and wild parties with naked women. I'd love to own a whorehouse. What a wonderful way to make a living." In their earlier hit song, *Bohemian Rhapsody* are these words, *"Beelzibub has a devil set aside for me."* Freddie Mercury said, "On stage, I am a devil." The word "queen" is homosexual jargon for a male homosexual. The song,*We are the Champions,* is claimed to be the theme song for the gay liberation movement. The song, *Get Down, Make Love* exploits homosexual relations in explicit terms. Another song is entitled, *All Going Down to See the Lord Jesus.* Pure Blasphemy!

Quiet Riot - Kevin Dubrow of the band explained what kind of crowd they attract: "The kids who come to see *Quiet Riot* are a lot like *Quiet Riot.* They're rebellious . . . We're the oldest juvenile delinquents in the world . . . They're rebellious, crazy people who want to party, get crazy and don't want anyone to tell them they can't

Quiet Riot

get wild . . . ." I wonder if really it is just that type of
teenager that is attracted to *Quiet Riot* or if, in fact, the
teenager that is attracted to *Quiet Riot* is encouraged to
become that way. One of their songs seems to hint at
that. Here's *Scream and Shout*: "*Scream and Shout .
. . Loose your mind and let it out . . . Your brains are
in our power, we conquer as we feed . . . A healthy
dose of metal is all you'll ever need . . . .*" If they are
programming minds as they claim to be doing in that song
off their *Condition Critical* LP, the product will be stripped
of all the morality and decency that put this country where
it is today. You see, *Quiet Riot* is a very popular group
among America's youth. The album, *Metal Health* sold
over five million copies! On that album is the song, *Let's
Go Crazy*: "*Lookin' for some action, wanna mean
machine . . . Gettin' hot and nasty . . . Climbing in between
. . . I'm gonna find a mamma that makes me feel alright
. . . Wanna kiss your lips, not the ones on your face
. . . .*" During one concert, Kevin Dubrow shouted, "I
hear people in New York are real nasty, and that you
like to do nasty things in the back seats of cars." What
is it like after a concert? "When we get off stage, we run
up and down the hallways naked and slap girls around."

(Video Rock Stars, 5/85) Dubrow said, "As far as this drug business, I mean, everybody in rock 'n' roll does drugs." (Tiger Beat, 1/85) Is it any wonder that the drug problem in America has reached epidemic proportion?

Rainbow - This group is or was led by the former lead singer of the legendary band "Deep Purple", Ritchie Blackmore. (At the time of this writing, *Deep Purple* released a new album.) Ritchie says that he holds seances in order to get closer to god. His god is an occultic one. Here is what he said when he told *Circus* magazine what the ideal conditions for holding a seance are, "You can't be very tired. And you can't have weak personalities present; otherwise, you'll get possession. You need very strong receptive personalities . . . ." Then he told of a friend of his who didn't believe in it. The friend told the spirits that he was stronger than them. The next moment he was knocked out of his chair and was foaming at the mouth. (Circus, 4/30/81, p.46) He also claims to the occultic practice of "astro-projection" (self leaving the body) during concerts to float over himself while he is performing. He records in a seventeenth century castle that is supposedly possessed by a demon that is a servant to the Babylonian god, Baal.

Ratt

Ratt - They took their name from a one bedroom apartment that they said was rat infested. Robbin Crosby said concerning that apartment, "You should have seen how hard it was to have sex down there." The 1985 smash top ten hit, *Lay It Down*, talks of their sexual sentiments: *"I know you don't really know me. I know you don't really care . . . You know you really want to Lay—it down . . . Under the sheets you will find me. I know that nothing's for free. You take what's good for your pleasing, I'll take what's good for this crazy evening . . . Lay it down . . . ."* When Crosby was asked what life on the road was like he replied, " Sodom and Gomorah." Remember what God did with Sodom and Gomorah?

Rolling Stones - In 1966 the *Rolling Stones* appeared on the Ed Sullivan Show to sing their hit, *Let's Spend the Night Together*. At that time, however, we had a fairly moral country, so they wouldn't let them sing that one. They had to change the words to, "Let's spend some 'time' together." A few years later, they released the album, *His Satanic Majesties Request*. On the cover, the members of the group were dressed as warlocks. In those days, *Newsweek* called Mick Jaggar "The Lucifer of Rock", "The Unholy Roller" and spoke of his "demonic power to affect people." (Newsweek, 1/4/71) Another album is entitled, *Goat's Head Soup*. In the next section of this book we will learn how the goat's head has, for years, been a symbol used in the occult for the devil. Some of their songs include, *Sway*—about demon power. *Dance with Mr. D* is about a dance with the devil in the graveyard at midnight, and *Sympathy for the Devil* is now the theme song for Satanic churches around the world. When they recorded the latter song, they went to an actual voo doo service and recorded the screams of people while they were being demon possessed. Those screams can be clearly heard on the song. Years ago at the *Altamont Rockfest*, the *Rolling Stones* hired the *Hell's Angels*, with drugs, to be their body guards. During the concert, the motorcyclists became so high that they went through the crowd knocking people over the head with pool cues. It was reported that some people died as a result of the blows to the head. At the culmination of the fest, while Mick Jaggar was singing *Sympathy for the Devil*, they dragged a man to the front of center stage and knifed him to death. Some believe it was a sacrifice to the devil. What did the Stones do about it? They filmed the ordeal and released it as a motion picture entitled, *Gimme Shelter*. Concerning the happening, *Rolling Stone* magazine said, "How could one of the Hell's Angels be held more accountable then Mick Jaggar for his incitement to Satanism?" Yet the *Rolling Stones* got away "scott free." Members of the *Rolling Stones* have a history of close contact with the occult. One of the foremost warlock satanists of this century, *Kenneth Anger*, was very closely associated with them. Listen to what he said about his friends, "I believe that Anita (girlfriend of both deceased Brian Jones and Keith Richards) is, for want of a better word, a witch . . . the occult unit within the Stones was Keith and Anita . . . and Brian. Brain was a witch, too. I'm convinced. He showed me his witch's 'tit.' He had a supernatural tit in a very sexy place on his inner thigh. He said: 'In another time they would have burned me.'" (David Dalton, *The Rolling Stones*, P.111) About the man who just spoke, Richards said, "Kenneth Anger told me I was his right hand man . . . once you start, there's no going back . . . ." (David Dalton, *The Rolling Stones*, p.38) Keith, by the way, does most of the music writing for the Stones. He said this about the music he composes, *"Songs come spontaneously like inspiraiton at a seance."* He explained how he was only a "medium through which the songs arrive." There is little doubt as to what is the source of rock and roll. Mick Jaggar has done some solo work. His most recent hit was entitled, *Lucky in Love.* In that song he sings, *"And late at night I lay in bed with a pistol to my head."* One of their new albums is called, *Undercover.* The jacket pictures a stripper with her private parts covered with stickers. The same album is full of sex. *She Was Hot* says: *"She was hot as she kissed my mouth . . . She pinned me to the ground . . . And she tore my clothes . . . I was lost in her burning flesh . . ."* *Tie You Up* says: *"You dream of it passionately, you even get a rise from it, feel the hot cum dripping on your thigh from it. Why so divine . . . The pain of love?"* As seen time after time, sexual themes go hand in hand with Satanic themes. This group is a good illustration of that truth.

Linda Ronstadt - She posed as a witch on the back of her first *Greatest Hits* album. She said, "I perform best with a shot of smack (heroin) in each arm . . . ." (Rolling Stone, 3/27/75) Her song, *Marquirita*, says, *"I'm all strung out on heroin on the other side of town."*

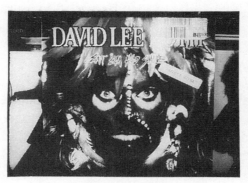

David Lee Roth

David Lee Roth - David Lee Roth was once the lead singer and perhaps the foremost member of "Van Halen." Many said that once he left the group, neither he nor *Van Halen* would do well. The opposite has happened. Both are making millions. Roth once said, "Whatever your vice, whatever your sexual ideals, whatever somebody else can't do in his 9 to 5 job, I can do in Rock and Roll. When I'm on stage, my basement facilities take over completely." He also said, "That's one of the reasons I'm in this job: to exercise my sexual fantasies. When I'm on stage, it's like doing it with 20,000 of your closest friends." (Rolling Stone, 9/4/80, p.23) *Musician Magazine* quoted him as saying, "I may not go down in history, but I will go down on your little daughter." (Musician Magazine, 6/84, p.52) Roth has a paternity insurance policy. Paternity insurance is a policy you can take out to protect yourself from being liable of any illegitimate children. Roth's latest LP is entitled, *Eat 'Em and Smile.* He is outfitted as a cannibal on the cover of the album. *There is a growing trend today towards cannibalistic themes in Rock.* Gene Simmons (*KISS*) was perhaps the initiator of it but others have continued it. There is even a group entitled, "The Fine Young Cannibals." *Why the alarm? Because demonism and cannibalism go hand in hand.* There have been in recent times, occurrences of cannibalism connected with the occult in America, yes America.

Rush - The term is drug related, short for "head rush." Their "logo" is a "pentagram" with a circle around it— identical to the pentagram used in witchcraft. Songs are very fantastical with reoccurring themes from Babylon and Egypt. (Something ABC news recently said was also associated with the surge of occult related crimes today.) One song is entitled, *Across the Styx.* "Styx" is the name

Rush

of the mythological river that runs into hell. Witches believe in reincarnation and that the crossing of the river Styx is one of the first stages of reincarnation. (Rock 'n' Roll and the Occult, Harrisburg, PA) Another song is entitled, *Necromancer*. Necromancy is occultic contact with the deceased. The song, *By-Tor and the Snow Dog* has a low rumbling voice giving these words, *"I want your mind and body . . . I want you . . . I am By-Tor."*

Santana - Carlos Santana said, "I am the string and the supreme is the musician . . . when I'm really in tune with the supreme, my guru and my instrument, forget it man, cause it's totally beyond anything—that's where I want to be." Two of his songs are: *Black Magic Woman* and *Evil Ways*. The song, *Abraxas* is about the foremost demon spirit.

Scorpions - This group is increasing in popularity among the ranks of the heavy metal bands. They have an album entitled, *Virgin Killer*. The original cover to the album featured a young girl (approx. 10 years old) on the cover, naked, with her legs spread apart and arrows pointing to her private parts. The words "Virgin Killer" were

Scorpions

plastered across the top. The title song of their album, *Fly to the Rainbow*, was taken seriously by at least one 16 year old boy. He left these words behind in his suicide note after jumping 30 feet off an overpass onto Interstate Highway 40: ". . . I belong in a world full of mystic powers, rainbows in crystal raindrops." (Reference to the song *Fly to the Rainbow*) He went on to say, "I wouldn't mind if someone would write the *Scorpions* and tell them their no. 1 fan has left. Tell them I've 'flown to the rainbow.'" (The Raleigh Times, 2/13/86)

Scratch Acid - According to *Spin* magazine, "Scratch Acid songs are about husbands setting wives on fire and rednecks exterminating longhairs with their four-wheel-drive pickups and insects on tonight's fish dinner and humans being devoured alive or dead or decomposed. Scratch Acid music will kill you." (Spin, 10/86, p.24) The article went on to tell how the members of the group are honest to goodness normal everyday young men. Later the article said, "Yow's (David Yow of the band) lyrics delve into the ugliest, most obscene desires hidden within the human psyche, but he denies that he's an abnormally frustrated person." (p.25) The sad truth of that matter is that today, among our "raised on radio" teenagers, these "fellas" are not all that out of the ordinary. Because throughout their lifetime, that's the kind of message rock and roll has been sending to them.

Sex Pistols - The *Sex Pistols* are recognized by most to be the first "punk" rock group. While John Lyden (nicknamed Johnny Rotton because of his black rotting teeth) and Sid Vicious are the names most often associated with this group, a man by the name of Malcolm McLaren is the strongest influence behind the band. To give you an idea what McLaren is like—prior to organizing the group, he was the proprietor of a shop in London named, SEX. In fact, he met Johnny Rotton in that boutique and first spoke to him about forming the new band there. They seemed to have become popular overnight, possessing little music value but their raw, leud and anarchist attitudes brought on the cult-like following they soon came to know. They actually "hit the limelight" by being banned in their homeland with the song, *Anarchy in the U.K.* Widely publicized incidents kept them in that fame, such as running a stream of profanity at a popular TV talk show host on national television. Another is the time Steve vomited on a woman in public. During the *Queen's Silver Jubilee* anniversary celebration, they released the song, *God Save the Queen, She Ain't No Human Being*. The sleeve had a picture of the Queen of Engalnd with a safety pin through her lip. Although they set a new trend in the rock world, one that has lasted to date and has united with the Heavy Metal scene, the *Sex Pistols* didn't last long. Sid Vicious was soon arrested for the brutal stabbing of his girlfriend. Released on bail, he was found dead as a result of a massive overdose of heroin. What did the pistols think of the American way of life? Malcolm McLaren sums it up well, "This band hates you, it hates your culture . . . You need to be smashed." (Rolling Stone, 10/20/77, p.73)

Slayer

Slayer - The album, *Show No Mercy* pictures the inverted pentagram and the Satanic lightning bolt *S* to spell out the name of the group. Also pictured on the front cover is a goat's head connected to a human body. Inscribed in the vinyl of "side one" are these words, "SATAN LAUGHS AS YOU ETERNALLY ROT."

Bruce Springsteen

Bruce Springsteen - An earlier hit, *I'm on Fire*, is about Pedo molestation. Here are some of the words. *"Hey little girl, is your daddy home? Did he go away and leave you all alone? I got a bad desire, I'm on fire. Tell me now Baby, is he good to you? Can he do the things to you that I do? At night I wake up with my sheet soaking wet. I'm on fire."* In *Cover Me*, he sings, *"Well I'm looking for a lover who will come on in and cover me."* Another earlier song, *If I were the Priest*, blasphemes Jesus Christ and the Holy Spirit. Making fun of Christianity is nothing unusual for Mr. Springsteen, he does so blatantly in concert. *People* magazine quoted him as opening concerts like this: "Welcome to the first church of the rock, brothers and sisters." He says that he was dead until "rock and roll" changed his life. In response to a screaming crowd he hollers, "Do you believe that if you die during the course of this show, due to excitement, that you're going to heaven?" He also makes mockery of a Christian testimony by telling stories of how he was going to become a baseball star "until rock and roll saved him." (People, 9/3/84, p.70) It seems as though he had some Christian roots but has rebelled against them. In the song, *Adam Raised a Cain*, his message is that just like the good Adam raised a bad

Cain, his good dad raised him. In the same song, he talks about the time he was baptized. Bruce was praised for his smash album, *Born in the USA*. On the cover he is pictured wearing all-American levis with the United States flag in the background. But the song, *Born in the USA*, is certainly not patriotic. If anything, it is a slap in the face to our country. The words of the song actually run America down for taking part in an attempt to free the Vietnamese in the Viet Nam War. On the same album he has another smash hit entitled, *Glory Days*. In this song, Bruce Springsteen glorifies drinking. In one verse he goes into a bar with an old friend and, over a couple of drinks, they talk about his friend's old baseball days. In another verse he visits a girl's house that he knew in high school. She was a "knockout" as a teenager, but is now divorced and has a couple of kids. Bruce sings that he went to her house and they drank together. Then in the last verse he sings, *"I'm gonna go to the well (tavern) tonight and I'm gonna drink until I get my fill."* In other words, he says he's going to go out and get drunk. Now it is sad that during the years of the Viet Nam War, 46,000 of our young men were killed. Let us remember—*though we may not all be happy with how things were done in that war, these men died for the cause of American freedom.* On the other hand, during the same years of the Viet Nam War, the war that Mr. Springsteen is criticizing in *Born in the USA*, over 250,000 innocent people were killed because of the same substance that Bruce is glorifying in *Glory Days*—alcohol. Both songs are on the same album. Where I come from, we called that "hypocrisy." Today our young people make a god out of the artist. Springsteen and the *E Street Band* released a record breaking LP "set" a few months ago. It is a five record set that charts Bruce's career from early fame to date in live concert recordings. The set is full of sex! In *Spirit in the Night* he sings about *"Janey"* with her hands in his crotch in the car on the way to the lake. When they got there they were *"makin' love in the dirt all night."* In *4th of July, Asbury Park (Sandy)* he sings, *"Chasin' the factory girls underneath the boardwalk where they promise to unsnap their jeans."* In *Growin' Up* he talks about staying high for a month at a time: *"I took month-long vacations in the stratosphere . . . ."* Later on in the same song he sings, *"The devil apppeared like Jesus through the steam in the street . . . I felt his hot breath on my neck as I drove into the heat. It's so hard to be a saint when you're just a boy."* In *Rosalita (Come Out Tonight)* he tells a girl to forget about what her parents say, but come on out and spend the night with him. He sings, *"The only lover I'm ever gonna need is your soft sweet little girl's tongue . . . ."* Many of the other songs are about sex. Due to the limited space we are not able to report on all of them. Others on the album glorify "a man running out on his wife", "a murderer is condoned though he shot a clerk in cold blood", and another song "glorifies running away from troubles." We learn something about the nature of the music when the most popular of them stoops to such depths.

Starship

Starship - Once a revolutionary group of the 1960's, they were known as *Jefferson Airplane*. Early in the 1970's they changed their name to *Jefferson Starship*. The group's popularity died out in the late seventies but today they are going strong having "dropped" the name *Jefferson* and are simply going by *Starship*. They are quoted: "The stage is our bed and the audience is our broad. We're not entertaining, we're making love." (Rock 'n' Roll, ACC Press, Tulsa, OK) While lead singer Grace Slick was married to Jerry Slick, she had an affair with her lead guitatist, Paul Kanter (now dead), and became pregnant. She often spoke of her concern for the health of the baby because of all the "weird drugs" they had been taking. When the child was born they named it "god." That's right, g-o-d, in blasphemy of the true God. *To many "rockers", their music is more than entertainment—it is their religion.* Craig Chaqico of *Starship* said, "Rock concerts are the churches of today." (Bay Area Magazine, 2/1/77) What kind of religion is this? In the *Long John Silver* album they blaspheme Jesus as a bastard that had an affair with Mary Magdalene. One of their hit songs in entitled *El Diablo*. In Spanish that means 'the devil.' The song says: *"El Diablo (or the Devil) I can feel your power in my soul . . . ."* That's what kind of religion it is!

Rod Stewart - This man has been known for years for his blatant sex in concert and song. One example of this is his hit *Tonight's the Night*. Tonight's the night for what? In the song he tells his girl to spread her wings so that he can come inside! Another of his songs is entitled, *I'm Gonna Kill My Wife*. Another is *Do You Think I'm Sexy*.

Rod Stewart

Styx - The name "styx" comes from Greek and Roman mythology meaning "the river that flows through hell." The group *Rush* has a song entitled, *Across the Styx.* All witches believe in reincarnation. They also believe that crossing the river Styx is one of the first stages to reincarnation. *Styx's* debut album pictures the group standing naked in flames and smoke as though they were in hell. Other albums include, *The Serpent is Rising, Crystal Ball* and *Equinox* (also the name of Jimmy Page's occultic bookstore in London). The album, *Paradise Theatre,* contains the written message on the cover that there is backmasking on the album. The song, *Snowbird* (about cocaine) backwards has these words, *"Oh Satan, move in our voices."*

Supertramp - *Supertramp's* latest album portrays evolution on the cover. They had a popular song some time ago that contained these words, *". . . you can laugh at my behavior that'll never bother me, say the devil is my Savior, I will pay no heed."*

Supertramp

Talking Heads - This group has a song entitled, *Heaven is a Boring Place*. They have an album entitled, *Speaking in Tongues*. Another album cover contains blasphemous remarks regarding God, the Bible and Christianity alongside caricature depictions of "so called" Biblical scenes. Tina Weymouth of the group said, *"Talking Heads* most popular song "live" is still Al Green's, *Take Me to the River*. It's got sex; cigarettes, which are a drug; Jesus; baptism; love; and nature, all in one song . . . ."

Talking Heads

George Thorogood - Alcoholic abuse is also a theme in rock and roll. *George Thorogood and the Destroyers* have a song entitled, *I Drink Alone*. *"I drink alone with nobody else, you know when I drink alone I prefer to be by myself. Now every morning just before breakfast, don't want no coffee or tea, just me and my good Buddy 'Weiser', that's all I ever need. The other night I lay sleeping, and I awoke from a terrible dream, so I called up my pal Jack Daniels and his pal Jimmy Bean, and we drank alone . . . ."*

Thrasher - This is another group that promotes the occultic violence of sado-masochism. Here is their song, *She Likes it Rough*: *"Shes loves the man who makes her bleed with pleasure. She'll do it all, she loves to surrender. All through the night she strains to get away . . . She likes it rough, she likes it tough, she likes it hard and mean. Tie her down, she knows what's waiting for her . . . Nothing too cruel, so beat her till she's red and raw. Crack the whip, it hardly stings the bitch . . . ."*

Jethro Tull - The back of the album, *Aqualung* says this, "In the beginning man created God, and in the image of man created he him. And he gave him a multitude of names, that he might be Lord over all the earth when it suited man. And on the seven millionth day man rested and did lean heavily on his God and saw that it was good . . . ." One song is entitled *Hymn 43*. It reads, *"Oh father high in heaven, smile down upon your son who's busy with his money games, his women and his gun . . . If Jesus saves well he better save himself from the gory glory seekers who use his name in death. I saw him in the city and on the mountains of the moon, his cross was rather bloody, He could hardly roll his stone."*

Tina Turner - This woman has made the news the last couple of years for her comeback after splitting up with husband, *Ike Turner*. Her comeback is largely due to the provocative sensuality of her promotion, stage show and songs. The album and song of the same name that highly contributed to her once again found fame was, *Private Dancer*. Here are a portion of the words: *"Well the men come in these places and the men are all the same. You don't look at their faces and you don't ask their name. You don't think of them as human, you don't think of them at all. You keep your mind on the money, keeping your eyes on the wall. I'm your private dancer, a dancer for money. I'll do what you want me to do. I'm your private dancer, a dancer for money, and any old music will do."* Her smash hit, *What's Love Got to Do with It* is a glorification of sex without any commitment. *Rolling Stone* put it bluntly, "Tina Turner is loose."

Twisted Sister

Twisted Sister - They have an album entitled, *Under the Blade* and another, *Beast*. One song is entitled, *Burn in Hell*. It reads like this: *"Welcome to the abandoned land, come on in child; Take my hand, here there's no work or play. There's just five words to say as you go* *down, down, down. You're gonna burn in hell. Oh, burn in hell.*" *We're not Going to Take It* was a hit video that depicted a young teenager who was not going to take being submissive to his father anymore. So he threw him down the stairs and out a second story window.

At the opening of many concerts, Dee Snyder, the leader of the group has said this: "There is an organization that can make your life better and it's not the moral majority. We're the people who don't want to be told what to f. . .in' do. Our organization is called the SMF, that's Sick Mother F. . .ers and if you follow *Twisted Sister* that's what you've got to be!" Yet in April of last year he had the "nerve" to say, "I was just like the kids today. I listened to *AC/DC* and *Black Sabbath,* and it didn't affect me one bit." (Hit Parader, 4/86, p.56) Those who glance at the picture might find a bit of humor in that statement!

Van Halen

Van Halen - An interviewer from *Rolling Stone* magazine after traveling with *Van Halen* for several days said this about the time he spent with the group. "I've seen enough nude women and heard enough graphic, abasing morning after anecdotes to fuel an article about porn-rock or a diatribe against sexism." (Rolling Stone, 9/4/80, p.23) Their

most recent album to date is called *5150*. '5150' means
"criminally insane" in police code. (Metal Hotline, 9/86,
p.17) That means *Van Halen* entitled their latest album
after those rapists, murderers and the like that pleaded
insanity in trial. Maybe that's what they meant with the
earlier song, *Running with the Devil*.

Venom - This group takes the satanic theme in rock to
the hilt. One album is entitled, *Welcome to Hell*. The front
cover uses the very same inverted pentagram with the
goat's head on the inside and Hebrew lettering on the
outside as does the cover of the Satanic Bible. Another
album is entitled, *Black Metal*. The cover of this album
pictures the devil himself with an inverted pentagram on
his forehead. These words are printed on the cover of
one of their albums, "Without any fear of God, we're
possessed by all that is evil. The death of you, God, we
demand. We spit at the virgin you worship and sit at lord
Satan's left hand." The following is just a sample of their
songs: *Son's of Satan, Welcome to Hell, In League with
Satan,* and *Possessed*.

Stevie Wonder - He has a song *Jesus Children of
America*. In that song he blasphemes Christ and ridicules
Christianity. The album, *Songs In The Key of Life* was
released to correspond with his astrological charts. The
album, *Inner Visions* depicts astro projection on the cover.
Astral projection is the occultic practice of self (soul)
leaving the body (picture from book is taken from the
occultic section of a bookstore).

W.A.S.P. - They are referred to as *Wasp* by their fans,
and they have many. *The initials stand for We Are Sexual
Perverts*. (Hit Parader) Blackie Lawless said, "I look at
Rock like a religion." (Faces, 2/85, p.53) Group member

W.A.S.P.

Chris Holmes tells how he came to join the band: "Blackie (leader of the group) saw my picture in the 'Beaver Hunt' section of Hustler Magazine." (Hit Parader, 4/85, p.74, 75) This is of no surprise when you listen to some of the words to their songs. Here are words to *Ball Crusher*: *"Such a wicked vicious woman, Black Voo doo Queen. Les-Bo Nymphomaniac, ooh she's got a girlfriend that's seventeen . . . ."* This is their song, *Sex Drive*: *"I got a message for you, it's something you love to do. You're thinkin' 'bout it all the time. You're lying in bed and it runs through your head, cause you can't get it off of your mind. You been thinking pink and you're loosing sleep, that rush is almost all you can stand. You feel it getting hard and your crotch starts to throb, it's body language you understand . . . I'm talkin' 'bout a sex drive it's everything you fantasize. Like a dog in heat, all dirty love is a treat."* One single they released was entitled, *Animal, F__ like a Beast.* It says, *"I got pictures of naked ladies lying on my bed . . . I whiff the smell of sweet convulsion . . . Thoughts are sweating inside my head . . . I'm making artificial love for free . . . I start to howl in heat . . .*

If__ like a beast . . . ." Sex and Blood have been the biggest part of their promotion and stage shows. Blackie Lawless became known for drinking blood out of a skull in concert. He also was noted for the fireworks and skillsaw blade that protruded from his crotch. He recently said, "We're through with the blood. We won't use it anymore on stage. Now we're moving on to new things that are even crazier. We're going in a more sexual direction now." (Heavy Metal Hot Shots, 11/86) When asked what the possible music trends of '87 would be, he answered, "Greed, lust and massive quantities of drugs." (Rock Express, 1/87, p.67)

ZZ Top - This group has been around for quite a few years. They recently hit gold again with the album, *Afterburner.* Called by some, *Rock's Bad Boys*, they live up to their name with this latest album. It is filled with double language for sex. The LP opens up with a song entitled, *Sleeping Bag.* The song invites a girl to *"Slip inside my sleeping bag."* The singer then explains what they will do: *"We'll tuck it in until it's clean out of sight . . . We'll look at some pyramids and check out some heads . . ."* *Woke Up with Wood* is about a man that woke up in the morning with an erection and what his "baby" did about it. The song, *Velcro Fly* says: *"Hey! Look at the hooks on your pants; makes you wanna dance . . . There ain't never a catch, all you got to do is snatch, do the velcro fly . . . You need just enough of that sticky stuff, to hold the seams of your fine blue jeans . . . Well, it feels so right when you squeezed it tight, you reach the end do it over again . . . ."* You can imagine what the song, *Dipping Low (in the lap of Luxury)* is about. The final song of the album, *Delirious* reeks in drugs.

Frank Zappa - This man is one of the most outspoken promoters of musical pornography. Here are the lyrics to his song, *Stevie's Spanking*: *"His name is Stevie Vai* (Stevie Vai is David Lee Roth's guitarist), *and he is a crazy guy. Last November, I recall, He needed a spanking. He decided then, a female specimen, would be exciting for a night to give him a spanking . . . She was large and soft, and she beat him off. Made him drool upon his dork and gave it a wanking after the spanking . . . ."* By many he is considered to be the unofficial spokesman for the rock and roll industry. He once said, "F... those people! . . . They don't know their a.. from a hole in the ground!" Another time he commented, "If you are opposed to this music, you are like a sick dog that needs to be shot and put out of its misery."

SYMBOLISM
and the OCCULT

What the album covers tell us.

Sybil Leek is called on the leaflet of one of her books, "the most famous witch in the world." She has pushed her religion through the medium of books, periodicals and nationwide TV talk shows. Some time ago, she was reported to say that many musicians put spells and incantations upon their music. In order to show that they have done this, they put some kind of a marking or symbol on that album. I know a musician in Hartford, WI who before he became a Christian, had been a rock musician who had "cut" several albums. This man told me personally that he had observed musicians doing what Sybil Leek refers to. According to this musician, after the "master" was recorded and mixed, the band members, along with part of the recording staff, would take the "master" into another room and place their hands over the recording. Then, they would incantate into the album, claiming to be casting demons into it. (This is a widespread practice among rock musicians.)

In this section of this book, we will take an indepth look at album covers as well as promotional material. We will also look at the major symbols used.

-2-

As you can see by picture (2), some groups are not shy about what they are doing. What are they saying with that statement? They honestly believe that they are receiving their fame from powers in the occult world—literally Satan. That is why we will see so much occultic symbolism on these albums. Bruce Dickenson of *Iron Maiden* said concerning the amount of Egyptian occultic symbolism on one album, *"The idea of "Powerslave" is to get enough magic on the album that it'd rub off on the whole event."* (Hit Parader, 4/85, p.4) He believed that by putting these symbols on the album, he would receive more power and success to gain popularity and fame! Notice something special about the above album cover. Notice the fancy way of printing the S. It is not just a fancy S, nor is it merely a lightning bolt. It is something quite common in the occultic world, something called a Satanic S, used to symbolize Satanic power. Its roots can be found in the Second World War with the Nazi SS. This was Hitler's elite core of men used to seek out and kill Jews. The idea of it comes from *Luke, Chapter Ten*, where Jesus told the disciples, *"I beheld Satan as lightning fall from heaven."* We see this same lightning bolt or Satanic S used time and time again. Here it is

-3-

-4-

(3) between the C and the D on *AC/DC's* album, *Who made Who*. If you read back on what *AC/DC* is all about, this is of no surprise. The song, *Hell's Bells* which is quoted in the previous chapter is also on this album. You can see it again on this *Alvin Lee* album (4). *Journey* uses it on their latest LP, *Raised on Radio (5)*. That one looks much like the one *Anton Levey* wears. We will see later that *Journey* uses a lot of occultic symbolism on their album covers. Here is the man (6) that said "Rock has always been the Devil's music." He has it imprinted across his face on his *Aladdin Sane* LP. A newly saved teenager

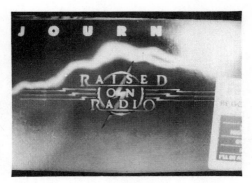

-5-

-6-

showed me how to break up that title, it says, "A lad insane." *KISS* uses it to spell out their name (7). In fact, for as long as I remember, *KISS* has done that on all their albums. It coincides well with the themes they use in their music.

The man on the left of the picture is Vinnie Vincent. He no longer plays with *KISS* but has done some solo work on his own. Notice the necklace (8) he is wearing. It is a cross with a loop on the top portion and is called an "Egyptian ankh." It is a fertility symbol having to do with the sun god *Ra*(9). The wearer of it was one who

-7-

-8-

-9-

practiced orgies. Today it has also taken on a reincarnation meaning. Many rockers wear the symbol. Notice that John Paul Jones from *Led Zeppelin* is wearing it (10).

-10-

In (11) Anton Levey is presenting some of the symbols used in his church. At the left is a skull to signify the constant reocurring theme of death. Around his neck is the inverted pentagram, which we will see time and time again. To the right is a crystal ball which, to them, is a strong medium of power. These also often appear on album covers.

-11-

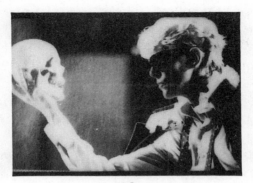

-12-

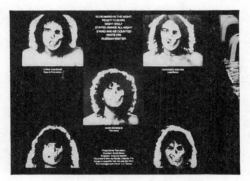

-13-

-14-

This is David Bowie (the same man who had the Satanic S across his face) in concert (12). Notice the backside of the album (13) where, half of each face is transformed into a skull. This *W.A.S.P.* album (14) pictures skulls, skeletons and the like, that they use during their show. This is *Judas Priest's, Sin After Sin* (15 & 16) both front and backside. Notice the skulls. *Krokus* features the skull and crossbones on album (17). Here is the earlier *Iron Maiden* LP entitled, *Killers* (18). The title is written in red to simulate blood(19). The demonic skeletal figure is the group's mascot and is made to look like one that has come back from the dead. Most of the songs on this album

-15-

-16-

-17-

-18-

-19-

deal in some way with death. This is the group, *Grim Reaper* (20) with the album, *See You in Hell*. The figure on the cover is the tarot (occultic fortune telling cards) figure of the Grim Reaper. *Blue Oyster Cult* (21) pictures likewise on the LP, *Some Enchanted Evening*. These groups are not alone in taking tarot card figures to use on their album covers. One of the most popular albums ever sold, *Stairway to Heaven* by *Led Zeppelin*, has the tarot figure "The Hermit" on the inside.

-20-

-21-

-22-

Drawing (22) shows some of the other figures the Egyptians used in their occultic activities. Pay particular attention to the beetle toward the bottom. It is called a "scareb." The same beetle is on the cover of album (23), *Powerslave* by *Iron Maiden*. Here *Journey* pictures it along with the crystal ball on the album, *Captured* (24). Again *Journey* uses both the crystal ball and scareb on another album (25). The lower and upper crystal ball is made to look like and could very well be simply planets. In no way is that bug in the middle a space ship! We see an-

-23-

-24-

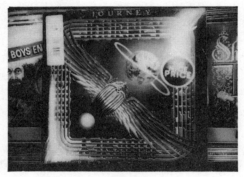

-25-

other symbol on this cover that we haven't yet discussed. Around the upper right planet is a strange orbit. Moons do not orbit planets in a figure eight, they do so in a circular motion. So what is that loop around the planet? We see the same figure in picture (26). It is a tarot card deck. The same "sideways" figure eight appears as a twisted halo over a person practicing witchcraft or magic. We are not sure what that symbol means (it stands for "infinity" in mathematics) but we do know it has some significance and *Journey* is not just playing a cute game. They are playing the devil's game!

-26-

There are still more tarot symbolism found on albums. The group, *Triumph*, has an array of tarot cards on their album, *The Sport of Kings* (27). This is a picture of the cover of a book (28) written to explain the magic use of tarot cards. On the cover is illustrated six of the cards used (there are many more). Each of the cards on this cover can be found related to some rock and roll album cover. *The Devil* pictures Satan almost exactly as Ronnie James Dio does on his album, *Holy Diver* (seen later). *The Hermit*, as mentioned before, is pictured inside Led Zeppelin's album, *Stairway to Heaven*. *Death* shows the inverted pentagram used by several groups, including the Grim Reaper pictured by *Blue Oyster Cult, Grim Reaper* and others. We spoke of *The Magician* earlier. The lower middle card is called *The Wheel of Fortune*. (Where have we heard of that before?) It is actually an astrology chart like the one on the backside of *Arcadia's* album, *So Red the Rose* (29). Notice that the second song on the second side of this album is entitled, *El Diablo* (30). A person

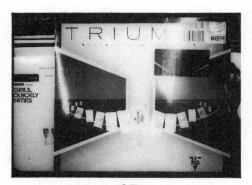

-27-

-28-

-29-

-30-

that knows Spanish will tell you that *el diablo* means, *The Devil!*

Astrology figures heavily in rock, and astrology involves much occultic activity. *Duran Duran* uses a lot of astrology symbolism in their material. The album *Seven and the Ragged Tiger* (31) was a "smash." It also employs quite a bit of symbolism. The upper right hand corner has an astrology emblem on it. The star is to symbolize *Lucifer*, and the moon, *Dianna*. The backside (32) is even more revealing. On the left side you see what looks like an upside down four combined with a two. The same symbol is located on this album by *Earth, Wind and Fire* (33). The same symbol is found in this occultic diagram (34). Going back to the *Duran Duran* album (35), at the top of the backside is the same symbol with an extra line added to it. Just below that and off to the right is something else. It is that same "sideways" figure eight that we saw on *Journey's* album and also on the tarot card—with a double cross on top. What is that symbol? What does it mean? Where did it come from? Those questions are answered by this picture (36). The exact same symbol is pictured inside the *Satanic Bible* under the heading,

-31-

-32-

-33-

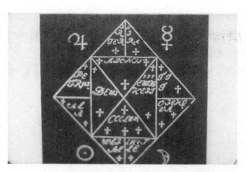

-34-

-35-

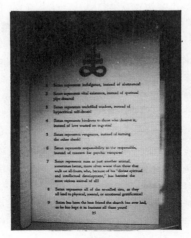

-36-

The Nine Satanic Statements. I don't know about you, but it alarms me to think that *Duran Duran*, one of the most popular bands in the land, perhaps the world, would have on one of their "hottest" albums a symbol taken directly out of the Satanic Bible.

-37-

Actually, the Satanic Bible is quite a popular subject in rock and roll today. The message of it is to do whatever you feel like doing, and don't let anyone tell you what to do; things like free sex, etc. This is also the message of the majority of rock lyrics. Some groups even copy the cover of the Satanic Bible on their album covers. This is the cover of the Satanic Bible (37) written by Anton Levey, the high priest of the Satanic Church in San Francisco, CA. This is the cover of *Onslaught* (38) by *The Force*. This is the cover of *Welcome to Hell* (39) by *Venom*. This is the cover of *Shout at the Devil* (40a) by *Motley Crue*. We see that the backside (40b) of the Satanic Bible has Anton Levey inside the inverted pentagram. What does *Motley Crue* do with the backside of their album? (41) They put themselves inside the inverted pentagram.

-38-

-39-

-40a-

-40b-

In the picture of Anton Levey, on the backside of his
Satanic Bible, you will notice that one of his hands is making
the "devil's tridad" or "Il Cornuto" sign (partially hidden
by the computer display). The two fingers pointing up
signify the devil's or goat's "horns." This sign is commonly
used in concert and pictures of group members on
promotional material. Fans are encouraged to show the
sign toward the stage saying it means "long live rock and
roll." If that's what it means, why is the author of the
Satanic Bible and pastor of a Satanic church using it?
If that is so, why was it used many years before rock
was around? To be truthful, "rockers" got it from the
occult and many of them use it because of the "power"
they believe it brings. In this picture (42), Gene Simmons
of *KISS* is making the sign language sign for "I love you"
with his right hand, and the Il Cornuto with his left hand.
Translated, that means, "I love you, Satan." The picture
was taken around the time Simmons wrote the song, *God
of Thunder*, quoted in the previous chapter.

-41-

-42-

-43-

As you noticed, both the inverted pentagram (which contains the goat's head) and the Il Cornuto sign are symbols for the goat's head which, in turn, is to symbolize the devil. The *Rolling Stones* had an album entitled, *Goat's Head Soup* years ago. In this picture (43), a member of the *Police* is posing with a goat's head on their popular album, *Synchronicity*. This album, *Hell Hath No Fury* (44),

-44-

-45-

(wouldn't the devil like teenagers to believe that), by *Rock Goddess*, has the skull of a goat's head pictured along with the three "group" members. *Heart* (45) has taken the gypsy scene as their background for the album, *Little*

Queen. (The gypsies kept occultic activity alive in America and Britain during the nineteenth century.) Notice the goat's head in the foreground. Is the goat's head really an occultic symbol? This ancient drawing (46) taken from occultic material would lead us to believe so.

-46-

-47-

On the backside of this album (47) we see Ann and Nancy Wilson with the same gypsy background. The dark-haired Wilson is holding forth a "crystal ball" just like the one Anton Levey held in the earlier photograph (11). The crystal ball has always been a symbol used in the occult. Many groups picture it. Stevie Nicks uses it often. Here

-48-

-49-

she is in *Bella Donna* (48) (also see previous chapter) with the crystal ball on the lower left. This sales record-breaking album with *Fleetwood Mac* (49) has her gazing at it. Her latest album, *Rock a Little* (50) has one on the lower right. Sheena Easton has two crystal balls on this album, *A Private Heaven* (51). Here is *Van Halen's* latest album and it too features the crystal ball (52). This is the backside of *Journey's Captured* album (53). The

-50-

-51-

-52-

-53-

-54-

front side was pictured earlier and it showed both the scareb and the crystal ball.

Closely related to the crystal ball is something called the "winged globe." There are several versions of it. Two are shown; one from *Journey's Evolution* (54) (notice also the twisted halo), and the other from *Aerosmith's Get Your Wings* (55).

The "pyramid" is another occultic symbol used frquently by rockers. Here is *Iron Maiden's Powerslave* album (56). As footnoted in the previous chapter, Dickenson claimed that the Egyptian theme was for the sake of getting "magic"

-55-

-56-

-57-

on the album. John Fogerty uses it here on his newly released, *Eye of the Zombie* (57). *Pink Floyd* (58) uses the pyramid. As seen earlier, *Earth, Wind and Fire* (33) pictures the pyramid.

-58-

Another symbol taken from Egyptian days and used in the occult is the "evil eye" (59). A documentary by 20/20 of 1985 referred to this as being present in Satanic rituals. It is found on at least two of *Iron Maiden's* albums,

-59-

Powerslave (60) and also their latest release, *Somewhere in Time* (61). The symbol is located to the left of the gun that the creature is carrying (62a). It is used over and over again on this *Allen Parson's Project* album (62b).

This is a book (63) on the occultic practice of "Rune fortune telling." These same figures are used on the archway of this Ozzy Osbourne album, *Speak of the Devil* (64), and on the border of this *Jethro Tull* album, *Broad Sword and the Beast* (65). You will notice that one of the runes is the lightning bolt or Satanic S.

-60-

-61-

-62a-

-62b-

-63-

-64-

-65-

We talked about the inverted pentagram, but what about the normal "five point star?" Surely, every time you see a five point star or normal pentagram it does not signify Satanism. No, but the pentagram definitely does not have to be inverted in order to be occultic. Actually, when it is inverted, the pentagram signifies black magic. When the single point is up and it is used as an emblem or symbol, it signifies witchcraft. The pictures (66),(67), and (68), all verifying this, are taken from occultic material. The circle around the pentagram gives extra credence to its occultic background. This picture (67), shows how

-66-

-67-

the *Rush* insignia (68) is definitely tied in with witchcraft. The naked man does bear significance when used with the encircled pentagram.

-68-

Some groups are simply blatant about Satanism on their album covers. *AC/DC* (69) is telling the world that the members of their band are on the highway to hell. Angus Young (called the guitar demon) is dressed up as Satan

-69-

and the now deceased lead singer, Bon Scott, is wearing a pentagram necklace. This *Black Sabbath* album (70) is entitled *Sabbath Bloody Sabbath*. Why is it a bloody sabbath? Because that girl lying on the bed with the serpent curled around her neck is about to be sacrificed to the devil! Notice the skull, the crystal balls, the nudity (as at actual Satanic services), the Satanic S's and the 666. *Blondie* shows the 666 being written on a man's forehead on the backside of the album (71). *Iron Maiden*

-70-

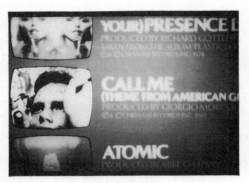

-71-

-72-

-73-

also used the 666. On the album, *The Number of the Beast* (72). The devil is pictured on the cover. He is pictured again in Ronnie James Dio's *Holy Diver* (73). On this cover, the devil is pictured much like the tarot figure shown earlier. With his left hand, the devil is making the Il Cornuto sign and with his right hand he is making the "peace" sign. But why the peace sign? The picture (74), taken out of pro-occultic literature, shows the

-74-

-75-

origination of that sign. Notice what the *DIO* spells when turned upside down (75). Ozzy Osbourne also likes to turn things upside down. On *Diary of a Madman* (76), he has the cross turned upside down, which is the symbol for human sacrifice. That's not all we see on this album cover. The little boy in the background (reportedly Ozzy's real son) is reading a book that is marked "SPELLS." On the wall is what appears to be an actual ancient witchcraft spell. That album may be more blatant than others, but not all that unusual. Linda Ronstadt (77) is posing as a witch on the back cover of her first *Greatest*

-76-

-77-

Hits album. On the cover of *The Wild Heart* (78), Stevie Nicks is dressed for and clearly acting out rituals of Black Magic.

-78-

We certainly are not able to cover all the symbolism used in the rock and occultic world today. However, this should suffice to convince you that it is real and it is going on. Sybil Leek was not just "blowing smoke" when she referred to the symbolism on today's album covers.

Did you notice how all these different groups, of different styles of rock, from different countries, backgrounds and cultures seem to come up with the same themes and symbols. Why is that? They are competing with one another, yet they use the same emblems to put on their covers. Why? The business world does not do that. *General Motors* does not use the same insignia that *Chrysler* uses and vice versa. *Pepsi* doesn't air the same commercials that *Coke* airs.

These groups are not coming up with neat markings to put on their albums to play games. Not on your life. They are serious about what they are doing! Their purpose in using the themes, the album cover illustrations, drawings and symbols, is more than trying to sell albums and make money. Many of these rockers honestly believe that there is power in these occultic symbols and that is why they use them. Many of them were told that by giving their music, albums and concerts over to the occultic world, they will be more successful, that they will receive "inside" help. To them, this is their life. They are not just playing around, they mean business!

The sad fact is that it is at your expense!

WHAT the VICTIMS SAY

These are the most neglected in the Rock and Roll controversy!

"Up until a couple months ago, rock and roll controlled me. I didn't realize it at the time, but alcoholics don't admit that they have a problem, neither do drug addicts. I came to realize it when I tried giving it up. It seemed like an impossible task, much harder than quitting smoking and drinking!"

—Tony

"When I started listening to rock and roll, I started to change completely! Eventually, my favorite groups came to be *Motley Crue* and *Quiet Riot*. I never started smoking (including dope), drinking or sex until I got into rock and roll. With it, my friends all changed and I started to get into trouble. If God would not have delivered me, I'd probably still be heading down the road that rock got me started on."

—Mike

"When I listened to rock music, I loved the loud sound that seemed to block out all my problems. I remember closing my eyes and swaying back and forth to the beat, occasionally letting out a loud "scream" to the music. It gave me the feeling that I could do anything I wanted to do! One of my favorites was *Shout to Thrill* by *AC/DC*. Listening to it made me want to rebel against everything and it started to make me think that there was nothing wrong with destroying other people's lives. I became very violent. All my heros used so much violence that I didn't think it was wrong to hurt other people. That's what eventually got me into so much trouble."

—Michele

"Rock would bring the anger out of me. After listening to certain songs, I would look for excuses to blow up at people and get into fights. I used to idolize Madonna. I wanted to be like her so bad that I started dressing like her in every way I could. Latter on, I got into *Motley Crue* and *Dio*. Then I started wearing headbands, spikes, ankle bracelets and things like that. I wanted to look like them, be like them and live like them. I'm so glad that Jesus Christ took me out of that. Now I've got something worthwhile to live for!"

—Lisa

"When I was small, I was always my "mamma's girl." Then I got into rock 'n' roll. The way I used to look at just about everything started to change. I didn't want to please my mom anymore, instead, I wanted to be like the rock stars I idolized. I remember really liking the song, *We're Not Gonna to Take It* (referring to a song by *Twisted Sister*), and thinking, 'Yeah, I don't have to listen to her all the time, who does she think she is anyway!' It got so bad that I started slapping my mom when I didn't get my way. I wish I could go back and do it all over again. I'd stay away from that music! It ruined my life."

—Mirella

"My favorite groups were *Motley Crue* and *Twisted Sister*. Listening to rock made me want to be rebellious. The songs made it seem cool to hate your family, so I did. My whole personality changed. Yet when I really got into rock and the things it made me want to do, I started to get so depressed. I wanted to quit at everything, especially life. I got so bad that I didn't even want to live anymore! Praise the Lord that He saved me and brought me to the place of real joy."

—Dawn

" 'Rock music has NO effect on me.' That's what I used to say. I sure don't say it anymore, I know what it did to my life. I was so blind, I did everything the music told me to do, yet I denied it had an effect on me. I started getting loose with myself. After a while I got very interested in a lot of the things they sing about. I started reading books on death, murder, sado-masochism, and watching psychopathic movies and things like that. I got the ideas from my favorite groups. I can't imagine what would have happened if I would not have gotten saved when I did. Yes, rock did have an effect on me. And it does on you too if you listen to it, no matter how much you deny it!"

—Tammy

"I used to listen to *Ozzy* and the *Crue* and sing a lot of songs about the devil and sex and drugs. I started to think that there was no God, only the devil and I should live for him. I thought that since these rock stars could do drugs and still make good videos, I could get into it too and be ok. They made me think that having sex was ok for me and that you didn't have to be married or anything to do it. But after I lost my virginity, I felt dirty and scummy. The rock bands didn't make me feel better then, only worse. When I was at the bottom, rock and roll didn't lift me up, the Lord Jesus did."

—**Jill**

"When I really got into rock, it seemed to control all my feelings. Some music gave me a burst of energy. Some made me want to fight with my mom and dad. Some made me feel real low. One such time I started to think about killing myself. I got a knife and carried it around all that day until one of my teachers saw me acting funny and looking at the knife. A song was going through my head while I was standing there and I felt as though I heard a voice inside me say that I could be popular, and people would read about me, and my parents would be sorry. My teacher, who was a Christian, came up to me just then and asked me what I was doing. The song seemed to fade away, and right there my teacher led me to the Lord."

—**Frank**

"My problem really started with soft rock. It started me on to harder stuff, but even the soft stuff put a lot of sex in my mind. It got to the point where all I thought about was sex. That's when I started listening to *Iron*

Maiden, Judas Priest, and groups like that. Soon my friends changed to looser guys and girls. I started partying, drinking and smoking pot. When I look back at when I was doing all that, it was the worst time of my life. I was miserable, and rock and roll is what got me started. Thank God I'm out of that mess."

—Michael

"My name is Derek and I'm seventeen years old. I come from a background of a broken family, drugs and heavy metal music. The devil wants you to think that this rock and roll and drugs and sex is all a party. Well I'm here to say it is no party! The devil is real, but so is hell! Pray today and ask the Lord to take your sin away and give you the life that is worth living."

—Derek

"Before I gave my life to Christ, I remember one *Ozzy* concert I went to with my friends. It got so "fired up" that we went to a party and drank half the night. After sleeping just a couple of hours, we got up and started drinking again. To make a long story short, we wound up joy riding while drunk, got into an accident and flipped the car."

—Chris

"I remember listening to rock for a long time with my friends. Then we would go out and look for fights."

—Bob

"The music I used to listen to affected me in an awful way. It used to cause me to get rebellious to the point where I wouldn't do anything my dad or mom wanted. My dad and I used to get into fights all the time. When I didn't like something, I'd go to my room and turn up my rock until I would get so mad I'd go and pick a fight. One time I beat my mother so bad it left bruises all over her. When I finished, I laughed in her face and told her to stop telling me what to do. I wish I would have stayed away from it. People say, 'well you were just like that, you would have done it even if you didn't listen to the music.' That's a lie, it was the music that made me feel that way and pushed me into doing it."

—**John**

"Rock and roll caused me to do things I had never before dreamed I'd do, I mean bad things! Just one incident that got me into more trouble than I'd ever been in, I don't know why I did it. I was staying at my grandma's house and was listening to a *W.A.S.P.* album. It just popped into my mind that it would be really cool to kill someone. I was mad at my grandma so I decided to kill her. I thought it would be easy since she took so many pills. She needed the pills bad and I knew it so I cut the telephone cord, and started throwing away all of the medicine of hers that I could find. I'm glad that I got caught before it was too late. People say that rock doesn't affect teenagers. I know how it affected me!"

—**Robert**

Does the Bible have anything to say about Rock and Roll?

In the story of "The Ten Commandments" (the one in *Exodus chapter 32* of the Bible, not the movie) Moses gets so furious that he smashes two tablets of stone against a rock and breaks them into little pieces. Now that's an ugly event to say the least. But when you consider that those tablets were the "hand-written work of God", delivered personally by God to Moses, you really have to wonder why Moses would do something like that. What was it that made Moses so mad?

Moses had been on the mountain for weeks receiving "The Ten Commandments". While he was on the mountain there had been an "uprising" taking place in the camp. The people were rebelling against God. They made a golden calf and returned to the worship of idols.

In *verse 7*, God told Moses to *"go, get thee down . . . the people have corrupted themselves"*, and in verse 10, "now therefore let me alone, that my wrath may wax hot against them, and I may consume them." When God says they have "corrupted themselves" and He is "waxing hot" against them, I'd like to find out why.

As he approaches the camp, Moses makes several very interesting observations. In *verse 17* we are told the people were "shouting." That in and of itself isn't significant, except that Moses then speaks of "noise of war in the camp." Since they didn't have "guns" or "bombs bursting in the air" to what was Moses referring?

All through history we read that "drums" or a "beat" has been associated with marching to war or war itself. Could it have been the beat of "drums?" I think so, and for more than that one reason.

Remember that the people were shouting? This was not the wailing and screaming of those being taken captive or of those who "shouted for mastery", even though that's the way it sounded. We read in *verse 18* that it was not the sound of those being "overcome" or "attacked" and "killed."

Verse 19 tells us that the people were "dancing" to this "singing" and drum "beat". In *verse 22* we are told of the mischief of the people, and in *verse 25* we read that the people had shed their clothes and were naked.

Could this have been the first recorded "rock concert?" Who knows? But we do know it was music or singing. We do know that the people had "corrupted themselves." They were naked, and . . . leave the rest to your imagination. We know the "singing" sounded more like "screaming" and "screeching." Whatever was going on was "bad news", because as you read on you will find that many people lost their lives.

Whatever it was that Moses heard was enough to cause God to say that those participating in it were corrupt. In I Corinthians 10:31 the Bible says, *do all to the glory of God.*

So, if you are one who attends rock concerts I make the following suggestion. The next time you head for a rock concert, take Jesus along with you. Or ask Him to "sit down and listen to your fovorite rock album with you." See if you can sit there comfortably, honoring the Lord, as you hear filthy lyrics, lewd gestures, Satanic references, drug taking and in some instances an "invitation" to sell your soul to Satan.

Does the Bible mention rock music by name? No. Does it describe a beat and a situation like most rock concerts today? You bet. God doesn't call "rock" by name, but He has a lot to say about the devastations rock music promotes.

Sex and drugs equals rock and roll. Rebellion, Satan equals rock and roll. Homosexuality, incest equals rock and roll. Sado-masochism, mutilation equals rock and roll. Suicide, alcohol equals rock and roll. Hopelessness, anti-godliness equals rock and roll. Murder, occultism equals rock and roll. The list goes on and on.

Much of today's rock music mocks, scoffs, and blasphemes everything God stands for. *The very sins that nailed Jesus to the cross are the themes of today's most popular rock music.*

In James 1:15 we read, *And sin when it it finished bringeth forth death.* Take a look at the list below to see how some of the rock "gods" have "fared."

Dead Rockers

John Belushi, singer of *The Blues Brothers*, died at age 32 in 1982, "speed balling" (mixing cocaine and heroin).

Tommy Bolin, of *Deep Purple*, died in 1975 at the age of 25. His death was also drug related.

John Bonham, drummer for *Led Zeppelin*, died in 1980 choking to death in his own vomit after downing 40 shots of vodka in 12 hours.

Brian Epstein, the manager for the *Beatles* died of an overdose of carbitol.

Pete Ham of *Bad Finger* commited suicide in 1975.

Gregory Harbert of *Blood, Sweat, and Tears* died a drug related death at the age of 28 in 1978.

Jimi Hendrix, guitarist-singer, died in 1970 at the age of 27 from a drug overdose.

Brian Jones, guitarist and founder of the *Rolling Stones* drowned in 1969 at the age of 26 while under the influence of both alcohol and drugs.

Janis Joplin, singer, died in 1970 at the age of 27 from a heroin overdose.

Paul Kantner of *Jefferson Starship*, now *Starship*, died of a stroke due to a lifelong ingestion of drugs, primarily LSD.

Bob Marley died from marijuana induced brain cancer.

Robbie McIntosh of the *Average White Band* died in 1974 at the age of 30 again as the result of drugs.

Keith Moon, drummer for *The Who*, died in 1978 at the age of 32, from a drug overdose.

Jim Morrison, singer, leader of *The Doors*, died in 1971 at the age of 27 from an apparent heart attack, brought on by heavy drinking.

Malcolm Owen, singer with *The Ruts*, died in 1980 at the age of 24, of a heroin overdose.

Elvis Presley, the king of *Rock and Roll*, died in 1977 at the age of 42 from a premature heart attack. Many attribute it as the result of extensive drug abuse.

Bon Scott, *AC/DC's* lead singer, the man who screamed the words to the song *Highway to Hell*, died of alcohol poisoning and suffocation.

Carl Radle, bassist for Eric Clapton died of a heroin overdose.

James Honeyman Scott, guitarist for the *Pretenders* died from a cocaine overdose.

Gary Thalin of the occultic English glitter band, *Uriah Heep*, died of a heroin overdose.

Sid Vicious, guitarist for the *Sex Pistols*, died in 1979 at the age of 21 from an overdose of heroin. This was during the time that he was being tried for the murder of his girlfriend.

Danny Whitten of the band, *Crazy Horse*, died a drug related death in 1972.

Alan Wilson of *Canned Heat* died as the result of drug abouse in 1970.

Paul Williams of the *Temptations* commited suicide in 1973 at age 34.

Suggested Reading

BACKWARD MASKING UNMASKED
Jacob Aranza   Huntington House Inc.

MORE BACKWARD MASKING UNMASKED
Jacob Aranza   Huntington House Inc.

TEENAGER, SOMEONE DOES CARE
Fletcher Brothers   Sword of the Lord Publishers

THE PIED PIPER OF ROCK MUSIC
Dennis Corle   J.B. Printing Ministry

THE DEVIL'S DISCIPLES
Jeff Godwin   Chick Publications

THE TRUTH ABOUT ROCK
Dan & Steve Peters   Truth about Rock Ministries

WHY KNOCK ROCK?
Dan & Steve Peters   Bethany House Publishers

Books & Tapes by Starburst Publishers

Horror and Violence—The Deadly Duo in The Media
Phil Phillips & Joan Hake Robie
(trade paper) ISBN 0914984160 **$8.95**

Turmoil In The Toy Box
Phil Phillips
(trade paper) ISBN 0914984047 **$7.95**

Halloween & Satanism
Phil Phillips & Joan Hake Robie
(trade paper) ISBN 091498411X **$7.95**

Turmoil In The Toy Box (formerly entitled *Deception of a Generation*) Phil Phillips
(90 min. video cassette tape—VHS only) 0006563589 **$34.95**

Deception of a Generation
Phil Phillips
(60 min. audio cassette tape) 0006563058 **$6.95**

Dungeons & Dragons
Phil Phillips
(60 min. audio cassette tape) 0006563775 **$6.95**

Spiritual Warfare
Phil Phillips
(60 min. audio cassette tape) 0006563449 **$6.95**

The Subtle Snare
Joan Hake Robie
(trade paper) ISBN 0914984128 **$8.95**

The Great Pretender
Rose Hall Warnke & Joan Hake Robie
(trade paper) ISBN 0914984039 **$7.95**

All listed books and tapes are available from your favorite Bookstore either from current stock or special order. You may also order direct from the publisher. When ordering enclose full payment plus $1.50 for shipping and handling ($2.50 if Canada or Overseas). Payment in US Funds only. Please allow three to four weeks for delivery. Make checks payable to and mail to STARBURST PUBLISHERS, P.O. Box 4123, LANCASTER, PA 17604. Prices subject to change without notice.